# TWENTIETH CENTURY
# INTERPRETATIONS

MAYNARD MACK, *Series Editor*
Yale University

NOW AVAILABLE
*Collections of Critical Essays*
ON

TWENTIETH CENTURY INTERPRETATIONS
OF

# SAMSON AGONISTES

TWENTIETH CENTURY INTERPRETATIONS

OF

# SAMSON
# AGONISTES

*A Collection of Critical Essays*

Edited by

GALBRAITH M. CRUMP

Prentice-Hall, Inc.  *Englewood Cliffs, N. J.*

A SPECTRUM BOOK

# Contents

# Introduction

## by Galbraith M. Crump

In *Samson Agonistes* Milton dramatizes for a Christian audience an Old Testament myth in the form of Greek tragedy. Thus because the play seeks to harmonize the traditions Milton was heir to, it has elicited a variety of conflicting critical approaches. Basically, they may be grouped into five categories concerned with (1) the physical and circumstantial similarities between Milton and his protagonist, and with (2) the play's sources, (3) its dramatic structure, (4) its spirit, and (5) its meaning. The present essay, while tracing the development of these approaches, will attempt to evaluate them and the light they throw on *Samson Agonistes*.

It is appropriate before looking at what others have had to say about the drama, however, to investigate briefly the origins of the work in Milton's mind, while recalling a few pertinent details of the poet's life. Milton was educated at St. Paul's School and Christ's College, Cambridge (1625-32), where his literary talents early manifested themselves. Following Cambridge, he continued his studies at his father's house at Hammersmith and later at Horton, Buckinghamshire (1632-38), before setting out on an eighteen month continental tour, spent mainly in Italy. Shortly after his return to England, Milton felt himself compelled to put aside his studies and poetic aspirations and enter into the political-religious struggle, writing in the Puritan cause against episcopacy. In 1649 he received the post of Secretary of Foreign Tongues to the Council of State. Though Milton's dreams of an idealistic society were shaken by the harsh practicalities of the Protectorate and his physical and mental health gravely impaired by the loss of his sight in the winter of 1651-52, he labored on at his post until the Restoration in 1660. The return of the Stuarts dashed his last hopes for the Puritan Commonwealth. As the regicides' apologist, Milton feared for his safety and went into hiding. In the summer of 1660 he was arrested and briefly imprisoned, but early in the autumn he was released, perhaps because he was no longer felt to be a threat to the government.

From that point, his career as public servant finished, he devoted himself to the completion of the great poems for which his previous life may be said to have prepared him.

The idea for a drama along the lines of *Samson Agonistes* had been in Milton's mind for a long time. Thirty years before the publication of the drama, the young Milton had recorded in the manuscript of his minor poems (now at Trinity College, Cambridge) a substantial list of themes suitable for dramatic composition. There Samson makes his first known appearance in Milton's work, and five episodes in the life of the Old Testament hero are set down for further consideration: "Samson in Ramoth Lechi" (Judges xv, alluded to in *Samson Agonistes,* 142-45); "Samson marrying" the woman of Timnath (see lines 219-26 and 381-87); "Samson *pursophorus,*" the firebearer, who drove three hundred foxes through the Philistine's corn with burning torches tied to their tails (Judges xv, 3-5, not referred to in the play); "Samson *hybristes,*" or in his arrogance; and "Dagonalia," the overthrowing of the temple of Dagon. These notations and their ultimate disposition when Milton came to write the play reflect the development of his ideas, as does another allusion to the Samson story of this period in *The Reason for Church Government* (1642). There he employs the image of the "mighty Nazarite" to define the present position of King Charles,

> who, being disciplined from his birth in the precepts and the practice of temperance and sobriety, without the strong drink of injurious and excessive desires, grows up to a noble strength and perfection with those his illustrious and sunny locks, the laws, waving and curling about his godlike shoulders. And while he keeps them about him undiminished and unshorn, he may with the jaw-bone of an ass, that is, with the word of his meanest officer, suppress and put to confusion thousands of those that rise against his just power. But laying down his head among the strumpet flatteries of prelates, while he sleeps and thinks no harm, they, wickedly shaving off all those bright and weighty tresses of his laws and just prerogatives, which were his ornament and strength, deliver him over to indirect and violent counsels, which, as those Philistines, put out the fair and far-sighted eyes of his natural discerning and make him grind in the prison-house of their sinister ends and practices upon him: till he, knowing his prelatical razor to have bereft him of his wonted might, nourish again his puissant hair, the golden beams of law and right; and, they sternly shook, thunder with ruin upon the heads of those his evil counsellors, but not without great affliction to himself.[1]

[1] *Prose Selections,* ed. Merritt Y. Hughes (New York: The Odyssey Press, 1947), pp. 144-45.

It is in the same tract that Milton discusses his own hopes, for which "time serves not now," of achieving for England "what the greatest and choicest wits of Athens, Rome, or modern Italy, and those Hebrews of old did for their country." Expanding on this idea, Milton compares the "doctrinal and exemplary" values of the diffuse, Homeric epic, or the brief epic patterned after the Book of Job, with "those dramatic compositions, wherein Sophocles and Euripides reign."

Clearly the emphasis of Milton's ideas has shifted quite radically by the time of his writing *Samson Agonistes*. Though the didacticism remains, it is now subordinate to the tragic rhythm and ironic mode that give it force. In his preface, which Thomas Warton read as Milton's apology to his "brethren" for having written a play, a form held by Puritans "in the greatest abhorrence," [2] Milton emphasized his indebtedness to classical tragedy. And though he mentions that *Samson Agonistes* was never intended for the stage, he stresses its economy of plot and purity of form in relation to its models. In dramatic incident, the play merely alludes to the youthful exploits of the protagonist, concentrating on the moments immediately prior to Samson's final confrontation with the Philistines. Thus Milton achieves a powerful unity in the externals of time, place, and action and centers the dramatic emphasis on the internal struggle of his hero to throw off despair and act with faith in "the living God." Essentially, Samson stands alone at the beginning of the play, in his despair unable to comprehend anything but himself. The entry of a group of his fellow tribesmen provides an appropriate choric background of consternation and grief as well as the first and mildest of a series of shocks to the former champion's disordered state. Increasingly violent encounters follow between Samson and his father Manoa, his wife Dalila, and the Philistine's strongman Harapha. Milton has shifted the action forcefully toward a revelation of Samson's mental state in response to these encounters (an emphasis that Dr. Johnson could not understand in structural terms, thus leading him to say the play lacked a "middle"). As a result of this shift, the plot and protagonist lose much of the allegorical quality they had for Milton earlier in his career, and Samson's final decision to end his struggle in grim play before the Philistines becomes something very close to a symbol of man struggling to escape the "Dungeon" of his being (*Samson Agonistes*, l. 156) and define himself within the vast dimensions of a theocentric universe.

The religious commonplace that the "real darkness of the body" im-

---

[2] Milton's *Poems* (London, 1785); cited by the Rev. H. J. Todd, *Poetical Works of John Milton* (London, 1801), IV, 339.

prisons the soul (*Samson Agonistes,* 156-59) has universal application, of course, but contemporary readers of the play at once perceived
its particular appropriateness to Milton. Writing commendatory verses
for the second edition of *Paradise Lost* in 1674, Andrew Marvell said
that when he "beheld the Poet blind . . . his vast Design unfold" he
feared

> That he would ruine (for I saw him strong)
> The sacred Truths to Fable and old Song
> (So Sampson groap'd the Temples Posts in spight)
> The World o'erwhelming to revenge his sight.

In the eighteenth century John Upton noted the autobiographical and
political implications by pointing out that Samson, "imprisoned and
blind, and the captive state of Israel, livelily represent our blind poet
with the republican party, after the Restoration, afflicted and persecuted." [3] Almost one hundred and fifty years later David Masson elaborately expanded on these hints, making them his own. In his view,
the "story of Samson must have seemed to Milton a metaphor or al-
legory of much of his own life in its later stages." Masson traced in the
poem, among other things, "the consequences of Milton's unhappy
first marriage." And though he did not go as far as Warburton had,
who in a typically foolish observation saw the play as "a satire on bad
wives," he was willing to presume that,

> although his two subsequent marriages were happier, the recollection of
> his first marriage (and it was only the wife of this first marriage that he
> had ever *seen*) seems always to have been a sore in Milton's mind, and
> to have affected his thoughts of the marriage-institution itself, and of the
> ways and character of women.[4]

Masson exploits the biographical approach to Milton, yet there is no
reason to doubt that the poet too saw himself reflected in Samson and,
as I shall suggest later, used the parallel to advantage. Among the ideas
that have collected about the poem, however, this one has perhaps received undue emphasis. It endangers the poem by tending to shift our
interest from the realm of art to that of psychology. Yet, employed perceptively, as it is by James Holly Hanford in his article printed below,
this approach remains one of the indispensable keys to the poem.

    [3] John Upton, *Critical Observations on Shakespeare* (London, 1748), p. 144.
    [4] David Masson, *The Poetical Works of John Milton* (London: The Macmillan
Co., 1879), III, 87-88.

Though eighteenth-century editions of *Samson Agonistes* stressed the investigation of its biblical and classical sources, identifying a host of references and allusions, this aspect of the play appealed to critics less than the study of its dramatic structure. Samuel Johnson launched the first major attack on the play from this point of view. Writing in *The Rambler* (no. 139, July 16, 1751) with his customary perverse perceptiveness, he conceded that the poem had

> a beginning and an end which Aristotle himself could not have disapproved, but it must be allowed to want a middle, since nothing passes between the first act and the last that either hastens or delays the death of Samson.

He continued in that essay to find fault with the "unsuitableness of thoughts to the general character of the poem," and with the "harsh and dissonant" versification in the choruses. When he came to write his *Life of Milton,* he returned to these complaints, expanding on them, and added that

> Milton would not have excelled in dramatic writing; he knew human nature only in the gross and had never studied the shades of character nor the combinations of concurring or the perplexity of contending passions. He had read much and knew what books could teach, but had mingled little in the world. . . .

In sum, then, Johnson found the choruses distracting, the plot and characterization deficient, and the structure inadequate. Insensitive to the excellence of *Samson Agonistes* though he was, Johnson focused attention on four aspects of the poem that required careful examination if it were to be fully understood and appreciated. By his animus, however, Johnson earned himself the role of criticism's whipping-boy among those who appreciated the play. One of the first to inflict stripes was the dramatist Richard Cumberland, who sarcastically challenged Johnson's high critical authority in *The Observer* (no. 76, 1784). Though Cumberland defended Milton's use of the chorus, the true importance of his reply to Johnson lay in his demonstration that indeed the play had a suitable middle:

> The death of Samson I need not describe. It is a sudden, momentary event. What can hasten or delay it, but the will of the person, who by an exertion of miraculous strength was to bury himself under the ruins of a structure in which his enemies were assembled? To determine that will depends upon the impulse of his own spirit, or it may be upon the

inspiration of Heaven. If there be any incidents in the body of the drama which lead to this determination and indicate an impulse, either natural or preternatural, such must be called leading incidents, and those leading incidents will constitute a middle, or in more diffuse terms, the middle business of the drama.

Thus the lines of battle over the dramatic structure of *Samson Agonistes* were drawn. Though it may surprise some readers, Johnson's position has continued to find adherents down to the present. But the persistence of the antagonists has aroused diverse and stalwart defenders.

Attempts to define "the middle business of the drama" have produced, directly and indirectly, a host of studies on the development of action in relation to Samson's character. Action is, of course, the key word here. Samson's progress from self-pity and despair to a recognition of his own responsibility for his fall and to his humble confidence "in the living God," is presented as psychomachia, an internal struggle toward self-knowledge, ultimately realized in the final "act" of death. In place of physical action, Milton builds the tension between the potentiality of action and the intensities of verbal and intellectual expression. In this he achieves the tone, or "spirit," of classical tragedy. Though such "spirit," as William R. Parker shows below, includes a strongly didactic strain, this is often subordinate, it seems to me, to purely emotional intensity. Against the calm lyric and liturgical beauty of the chorus, the tragedian sets verbal encounters of such tension that they must of necessity be brief. Their intensity cries out, at times, for the release of mere physical action—the sight of the death blow itself would be more welcome than Agammenon's shriek. In this sense, though Samson's meeting with Dalila may be the most dramatic in the play, the encounter with Harapha brings the potential for physical action to its peak before the climax. Here, at a moment when physical violence seems the only possible result of the confrontation, Samson achieves instead a nearly perfect mastery of his passions. Throughout the play, as in classical tragedy, the tensions produced by irony are augmented by the parallel set of tensions established between potential physical violence and its restraint.

On the question of the choruses Johnson met with less resistance from Cumberland. The latter offered a reasonable explanation of the function of the chorus in classical drama, but he did little to justify Milton's using it. He felt that "by casting out of his composition the strophe and antistrophe," Milton had robbed the choruses of "that lyric beauty, which he was capable of bestowing in the highest perfection." Critics generally agreed with Johnson and Cumberland about the versification of the poem and, in particular, of the choruses. Though Bishop Hurd spoke up for the so-called "ungrammatical" style and "licentious" meter of the play, saying that the "irregular construction carries with it an air of negligence well suited to his drama, and yet prevents the expression from falling into vulgarity," adding the notion that "a looseness of measure gives grace and ease to the tragic dialogue," his voice was in the minority. So much was this true that, believing Milton to have learned his "secret" as a result of diligent study of the Greek tragedians, especially Euripides, Hurd cautioned critics who were "perpetually tampering with Milton's careless expression, careless numbers, etc.," because they were "unconscious that both were the effect of art."[5]

Despite Bishop Hurd's warning, it was not until the nineteenth century that the metrics of the poem received detailed and sympathetic analysis from Gerard Manley Hopkins. Writing to Bridges in 1877, ten years before the latter's essay on *Milton's Prosody* first appeared, Hopkins linked Milton's experimentation with "accentual counterpoint," particularly in the choruses of *Samson Agonistes,* to his own sprung rhythm:

> The choruses . . . are intermediate between counterpointed and sprung rhythm. In reality they are sprung, but Milton keeps up a fiction of counterpointing the heard rhythm (which is the same as the mounted rhythm) upon a standard rhythm which is never heard but only counted and therefore really does not exist. The want of a metrical notation and the fear of being thought to write mere rhythmic or (who knows what the critics might not have said?) even unrhythmic prose drove him to this. Such rhythm as French and Welsh poetry has is sprung, counterpointed upon a counted rhythm, but it differs from Milton's in being little calculated, not more perhaps than prose consciously written rhythmically, like orations for instance; it is in fact the *native rhythm* of the words used bodily imported into verse; whereas Milton's mounted rhythm is a real poetical rhythm, having its own laws and recurrence, but further embarrassed by having to count.[6]

What Hopkins had discovered, Bridges went on in *Milton's Prosody* to elaborate, concluding that Milton was not "inventing anything new or unheard, but seeking rather to make good use of natural English

[5] Cited by Todd, 1842 edition, III, 324-25.
[6] *The Letters of Gerard Manley Hopkins,* ed. Claude C. Abbott (London: Oxford Univ. Press, 1935), pp. 45-46.

stress rhythms." The difference between Hopkins and Bridges lay in the degree of originality each allowed Milton. Whereas both spoke of the natural or native stresses Milton employed, Bridges characteristically attempted to draw this into the common vein, while carefully expounding his ideas on accentual verse. In the process, Bridges decried those lofty poetic natures in Milton's day who had thought trisyllabic verse "beneath their style." As a result, he rewarded Milton with a certain popular acceptability.[7] For Hopkins, however, the choruses offered yet another proof of Milton's originality and daring.

The highly individual patterns of *Samson Agonistes* have continued to engage critics and scholars to the present. Most have agreed to link the style of the play with the plain, middle style of *Paradise Regained* as distinct from the ornate, high style of *Paradise Lost*. Several have seen a connection and possible explanation for the new emphasis on plainness in the famous dismissal by Jesus in *Paradise Regained* of "all the Oratory of *Greece* and *Rome*" for what "is plainest taught and easiest learnt" (IV, 360-61). The source of the prosody of the choruses has been sought in contemporary Italian drama, or melodrama, in the new interest in the Pindaric ode, and in the *canzone* of Italian pastoral drama.[8] James Holly Hanford says that the "variations from the iambic pattern are so great" that many will "consider them frankly as a reproduction of Greek and Roman rhythms." [9] Ernest Sprout feels, however, that

> any similarity to Greek rhythms may be due solely to the contrapuntal interplay of prosody stress and speech accent which is heard alike in classical quantitative and English syllabic verse, or, as Matthew Arnold suggested, [Milton] may have created in English the rhythms which produced in him an impression similar to that produced in him by the Greek choral measures. He did not write quantitative English verse in imitation of Greek and Latin hexameters. . . .[10]

As this summary of opinion suggests, the riddle of the choruses may not admit of satisfactory solution, but one possibility that well suits

---

[7] Robert Bridges, *Milton's Prosody* (Oxford: Oxford Univ. Press, 1921), pp. 65-66.

[8] Louis Martz, *The Paradise Within* (New Haven: Yale University Press, 1964); Gretchen L. Finney, "Chorus in *Samson Agonistes*," *Publications of the Modern Language Association*, LVIII (1943), 649-64; Edward Weismiller, "The 'Dry' and 'Rugged' Verse," in *The Lyric and Dramatic Milton*, ed. Joseph H. Summers (New York: Columbia University Press, 1965), pp. 115-52; F. T. Prince, *The Italian Element in Milton's Verse* (Oxford: The Clarendon Press, 1954).

[9] James Holly Hanford, *A Milton Handbook* (New York: Crofts, 1926), p. 324.

[10] Ernest Sprout, *Milton's Art of Prosody* (Oxford: Basil Blackwell, 1953), pp. 130-31.

the facts as we have them has received scant attention since it was proposed by Frank Kermode some fifteen years ago (see below, pp. 99). Discarding the normal emphasis on Greek, Latin, or Italian patterns, Kermode suggested that Milton was attempting to reproduce in the choruses the patterns of the Psalms, which the age considered, in Cowley's phrase, to be "the most exalted pieces of poesie." Though we know from his nephew John Phillips that "David's Psalms were in esteem with [Milton] above all Poetry," [11] the immediate objection to Kermode's theory stems from Milton's own remarks in the preface to *Samson Agonistes*. If he were attempting to reproduce the patterns of the Psalms, would he not say so instead of referring to his decision to avoid the regular use of "Strophe, Antistrophe or Epode" in the Greek manner? Kermode attempts to answer this objection by reminding us that Milton "tells us nothing whatsoever about the system of his choral verse except that it is not divided as the Greek tragedians divided theirs." [12]

To return to the summary of critical ideas that have grown up around *Samson Agonistes*, subsequent nineteenth and twentieth-century critics were generally content to discuss Milton's poem in relation to its structure and its classical tone. In 1908, however, a paper by the noted Hellenist, Sir Richard Jebb, was read posthumously before the British Academy. It challenged the poem's right to be considered Hellenic in spirit, proposing that though it "may fairly be called classical in language and structure," in spirit it was Hebraic. Jebb's pronouncement opened new vistas of critical debate. The fullest and most carefully weighed response to Jebb's position came from William Riley Parker in his book *Milton's Debt to Greek Tragedy* (1937), in which he brought together the results of a long period of thinking and writing

[11] Helen Darbishire, *The Early Lives of Milton* (London: Constable & Co., 1932), p. 33.
[12] Critics from Hopkins and Bridges forward have recognized that Milton presumably scanned and read his verse in two different ways (*Milton's Prosody*, pp. 17-18). A contrapuntal or accentual emphasis suits well with the habits of Hebrew poetry, which developed a complicated pattern of parallel members or "thought-rhythms" in which "every verse must consist of at least two 'members,' the second of which must, more or less completely, satisfy the expectation raised by the first" (Theodore Robinson, *The Poetry of the Old Testament*, London: Duckworth, 1947, p. 21). Though strictly speaking there is no meter, the beat of the Hebraic line is predominantly ascending. Hopkins' sprung rhythm is, at times, itself not unlike Hebrew thought-rhythm:

Earnest, earthless, equal, attuneable,/vaulty, voluminous, . . . stupendous
Evening strains to be time's vast,/womb-of-all, home-of-all hearse-of-all night.
(*Spelt from Sibyl's Leaves*, 11.1-2)

on the subject. The chapter that most directly deals with Jebb's concern over the "spirit" of the play is reprinted below, but, as Arnold Stein recently pointed out, the question continues to have pertinence:

> perhaps in addition to studies of the Hellenistic and Christian traditions back of this poem we could use a "modern" study of Milton's "Hebraism"—not an assessment of his knowledge but of his understanding. Such a study would begin by usefully excavating Matthew Arnold's old position.[13]

An obvious alternative to either Hellenic or Hebraic theories defines the poem in a Christian context. F. Michael Krouse was the first scholar to attempt a comprehensive study of this background. In *Milton's Samson and the Christian Tradition* (1949), he evaluates the interpretations of and commentaries on the Samson story by patristic and scholastic exegetes who saw the Old Testament folk-hero as a prefiguration of Christ. Though Krouse's work is primarily historical and perhaps too heavily weighted in its point of view, it has had an unquestionable influence on later attempts to read *Samson Agonistes* as an essentially Christian play. A fair idea of the variety and complexity of these analyses may be gleaned from the present volume, much of which is given over to this question and related debate between Hellenists and Hebraicists.

In looking back over the varieties of critical opinion outlined above, we may remind ourselves that its diversity is both a tribute to and a result of the breadth and complexity of Milton's vision. Yet it must also be admitted that Milton's lofty nature has added to the partial eclipse his reputation suffers from time to time. It may, for example, lie behind what I have called the touch of animus in Dr. Johnson's estimate of him. Milton's emphasis on a complex vision rather than on a vision of complexities certainly contributed to the general disfavor his poetry aroused among the new critics between the wars. And now, after an all-too-brief period of renewed interest in his work, there are signs that his popularity is once more on the wane. His religion, like his style, feels unwieldy, and the intellectual demands his poetry makes on us seem to arise from his confusion of art and ethics.

It is precisely in these demands, however, that we confront Milton's greatness. His genius forced him into a kind of total engagement which would not allow him to do one thing at a time. He never looks at an

---

[13] Arnold Stein, *Heroic Knowledge* (Minneapolis: Univ. of Minnesota Press, 1957), pp. 227-228. See Stein's article reprinted below, p. 63, note 1.

object or an idea in a two-dimensional way, but, rather like the photographic process known as holography, from all angles at once. Graphically, my figure may best be applied to *Paradise Lost,* but conceptually, I believe, it works as well for the other great poems, particularly *Samson Agonistes.* So much gets into these poems that it becomes difficult for us to participate in them. As a result, we tend to work with individual planes or surfaces and try to construct a theory of the whole from some of its parts. The various aspects, in turn, become postulates of critical conflict and threaten to reduce the poem to a text *cum notis variorum.*

Alongside any summary of the attempts to determine the structural, thematic, or conceptual nature of *Samson Agonistes,* one might place the simple but often-overlooked notion of its very special kind of richness and density, which might be termed syncretistic. Like Spenser, but with a vastly different kind of intellectual rigor, Milton was a syncretist, believing that one must listen to the wisdom of all cultures and make it a profoundly valuable part of one's own heritage. The possibility of an "informational overload" would scarcely have occurred to Milton, nor should it to his readers. *Samson Agonistes* is at once Greek, Hebraic, and Christian in spirit; *we* have compartmentalized and caused the controversies. Milton recognized how inextricably the three cultures were tied together for him and his audience. Surely, he would have agreed with Matthew Arnold's essay on "Hebraism and Hellenism" in *Culture and Anarchy,* except for its minimizing of the role of the Reformation:

> As the great movement of Christianity was a triumph of Hebraism and man's moral impulses, so the great movement which goes by the name of the Renascence was an uprising and re-instatement of man's intellectual impulses and of Hellenism. We in England, the devoted children of Protestantism, chiefly know the Renascence by its subordinate and secondary side of the Reformation. The Reformation has often been called a Hebraising revival, a return to the ardour and sincereness of primitive Christianity. No one, however, can study the development of Protestantism and of Protestant churches without feeling that into the Reformation too,—Hebraising child of the Renascence and offspring of its fervour, rather than its intelligence, as it undoubtedly was,—the subtle Hellenic leaven of the Renascence found its way, and that the exact respective parts, in the Reformation, of Hebraism and of Hellenism, are not easy to separate.[14]

[14] Matthew Arnold, *Culture and Anarchy,* ed. R. H. Super (Ann Arbor: Univ. of Michigan Press, 1965), p. 172.

The dramatic structure of *Samson Agonistes* provides a case in point, where the complexities of Hellenic and Hebraic are welded together to meet the needs of a Christian audience. The form is undeniably Attic, availing itself of the conciseness of the classical drama and the tensions of tragic irony. In the choruses, however, Milton may have combined a Hellenic structural device with the feel of Hebrew prosody. From the sparse but strictly efficient development of plot he exacted an authority of form that embodies the recognition of the paradoxical Christian-Attic vision that worldly tragedy may bring a humility of self-knowledge that turns death into apotheosis.

Finally, if Milton believed, as Arnold did, that the "uppermost idea with Hellenism is to see things as they really are; the uppermost idea with Hebraism is conduct and obedience," he could scarcely have found a better figure than Samson to body forth the particular blend of those characteristics that were his cultural inheritance. Samson exemplifies man's struggle to be obedient and his achievement of vision out of blindness. Milton and his contemporaries saw in Samson a link, by way of the Hercules myth, with the Hellenic world as well as an Old Testament prefiguration of Christ. The likeness of Milton's own condition to that of Samson probably seemed to him, moreover, an added advantage. He had worked similar associations in *Paradise Lost* magnificently, particularly in describing Satan's journey from the depths of Hell into light at the opening of Book III. This passage is itself illuminated and enriched by cross-identifications between poet and antagonist, both newly "escap't the Stygian Pool," and by superb lyric ironies contrasts the inner light of the blind poet with the inner darkness of Satan's vision.[15] In the similarity of his fate to Samson's, Milton presumably saw not only the opportunity to assuage some of his own personal, political, and religious frustrations, but also the means to add intensity to his characterization of Samson. In reference to the protagonist, Dr. Johnson's remark that Milton "knew human nature only in the gross" does not apply. Who better could know and portray the agonies of Samson than one who might say justly of himself:

> I dark in light expos'd
> To daily fraud, contempt, abuse and wrong,
> Within doors, or without, still as a fool,
> In power of others, never in my own;
> Scarce half I seem to live, dead more than half.

[15] See Don Cameron Allen, "Milton and the Descent to Light," *Milton Studies in Honor of Harris Francis Fletcher, Journal of English and Germanic Philology,* LX (1961), 614-30.

Milton knew the agony and made it something much greater than private suffering by centering it in his Samson. Far from suppressing the lyric and personal vein in the narrative, Milton worked it exhaustively, recognizing in his own situation the means to give his play immediacy.

We are wrong, it seems to me, if we allow the autobiographical question to engage us in controversy, one way or the other. By so doing we restrict our understanding of the drama in yet another way by tending to overlook what Milton would never have forgotten—that his theme was at once Hellenic, Hebraic, and Christian, that it was old and new, general and particular, immediate and timeless, universally personal. Partisan in nature, like everything in Milton's career, it employs a tribal hero and tribal prejudices to increase dramatic impact, but then as now the play speaks first to the integrity of the individual in face of oppression and to the strength of one's convictions in face of doubt. Milton struggled to make *Samson Agonistes* embody all these and many more diverse points of view, because he knew that each in its way contributes to our knowledge of the vastness of the human heart in relation to the truth of its God and thus to its ability to triumph in defeat.

I wish to thank my colleagues Robert Daniel, Richard Henshaw, and William McCulloh and members of the staff of the Kenyon College Library, especially Virginia Clark and Peter Kidder, for their advice and assistance.

# Samson Agonistes and Milton in Old Age

## by James Holly Hanford

Paradise Lost, the "monumentum aere perennius" which Milton had planned in youth but whose execution he perilously delayed till beyond his fiftieth year, stood complete and glorious by the summer of 1665. Before its publication in 1667 its author had probably finished the second masterpiece of his maturity, Paradise Regained. The composition of Samson Agonistes presumably fell within the immediately succeeding years. The two poems appeared together in 1671. Were these later works really afterthoughts, as Thomas Ellwood's well-known anecdote regarding the first of them suggests? Despite the gentle Quaker's unquestionable candor I cannot think so. At his comment, "Thou hast said much here of Paradise lost, but what hast thou to say of Paradise found?", the poet sat in silence and seemed to meditate. We are under no compulsion to believe that he was struck dumb by the novelty of the idea! There is, to be sure, the later very explicit statement, quoted by Ellwood as made when Milton showed him in London the manuscript of Paradise Regained: "This is owing to you, for you put it in my head at Chalfont which before I had not thought of," but is it not quite possible that Ellwood is here innocently twisting some merely polite or even ironical remark of Milton's into conformity with his own self-flattering opinion that he was the "fons et origo" of an epic poem?

However this may be, there is a kind of inevitability in these last two works which makes it difficult to accept the idea that a chance suggestion in any very important way determined either of them. In form

"Samson Agonistes and Milton in Old Age," by James Holly Hanford. From Studies in Shakespeare, Milton, and Donne, by Members of the English Department of the University of Michigan, University of Michigan Publications in Language and Literature, vol. 1. Reprinted by permission of author.

and general character, at least, we may regard them as predestinate. The evidence goes back to a passage in the *Reason of Church Government*, written in 1641, where Milton takes the reader into his confidence regarding his literary ambitions. He is in doubt, he tells us, whether to adopt the form of an extended epic like the *Aeneid,* or of the brief epic which he says is illustrated by the Book of Job, or of drama, "in which Sophocles and Euripides reign." Since life and energy endured he did all three, taking thereby a triple bond of fame. *Paradise Lost* is the new *Aeneid,* exhibiting all the recognized technique of the full and perfect epic; *Paradise Regained* is something more unusual, a heroic poem composed entirely of dialogue, save for a narrative introduction and conclusion and a few links. Its formal precedent is obviously the Book of Job, regarded not as a drama but, more strictly, as a modification of the epic type. *Samson Agonistes,* finally, is Hellenic tragedy restored.

With his plan of life endeavor thus beyond expectation fulfilled, it seems unlikely that Milton would ever have considered a further addition to his poetical works. The lengthy list of dramatic subjects in the Cambridge manuscript (which includes a "Samson Agonistes" under the title "Dagonalia" and a kind of "Paradise Regained" under that of "Christus Patiens") together with the corresponding one of epic themes which Professor [Allan H.] Gilbert supposes him to have drawn up at the same time[1]—these lists were not in any sense a program. Milton was not given, like the dreamer Coleridge, to projecting vaguely a host of works which he could never write. The manuscript materials are notes taken in the process of canvassing the whole range of available materials before making a final choice. Had Milton enjoyed twenty more years of life and had there been twenty Ellwoods to urge him on, we should never have had at his hands the suggested epic on the deeds of Alfred, or the drama of "Sodom Burning" or the new Macbeth. To write any one of them would have been to mar the antique symmetry of his achievement.

It is not, however, from the standpoint of outward form alone that Milton had reason to regard his contemplated work as done. The three poems are complementary in theme and in ethical idea. Taken together they constitute a complete and unified embodiment of Milton's Christian humanism, the full working out of the didactic purpose

[1] Allan H. Gilbert, "The Cambridge Manuscript and Milton's Plans for Epic," *Studies in Philology,* XVI (1919), 172-76.

which he had accepted as a responsibility implied in his abandonment of the office of preacher for the more congenial one of poet.*

\*        \*        \*

It is now possible to consider the less obvious position of *Samson Agonistes* in Milton's poetic scheme. Formally and theologically the poem has no relation at all to its predecessors. For Milton does not, in his interpretation of the Old Testament material, adopt the point of view of the medieval religious drama, which built everything it treated into a single structure, regarding the events and characters of Hebrew history as episodes in an action which proceeded logically from the creation of the angels to the day of judgment. The story of Samson has for him an independent human value, neither implying nor prefiguring the life of Christ. For this very reason it adapts itself more naturally to his purposes, and affords the means of completing his representation of the state of man. The function of Christ we have already seen. He is, besides being the redeemer, the second Adam and the model man. But unlike Adam, Christ is without sin. Hence while he is the pattern and guide of human life, his victory is not, as ours must be, a recovery of something lost. The full account of man in his relation to the forces of good and evil demands another picture—the representation of frail humanity, burdened with the memory of former sin, but now repentant, restored to strength, and wrestling successfully with further trial. To what extent can *Samson Agonistes* be shown to fit this ideal prescription? The question raises some points of interpretation which appear to have been neglected by the numerous critics who, since Samuel Johnson, have discussed the merits of the work as drama.

When Milton, in 1641, first considered the life of the great but erring Hebrew champion as possible literary material and set down five subjects from it in the Cambridge manuscript, he was doubtless prompted chiefly by the coincidence of the story with characteristic themes of ancient drama. Samson was blind through his own guilt like Oedipus. In all other respects he was a Hebraic Herakles—the performer of incredible labors, enthralled by woman, sealing his baffled strength by a final destructive act. Such circumstances meant much in Milton's predisposition to a literary theme. More influential, however, in his final decision in favor of the subject was his perception of the

---

* A brief consideration of the relationship in theme and idea of *Paradise Lost* and *Paradise Regained* has been omitted—Ed.

parallel between Samson's sin and that of Adam. The point had already impressed itself upon him when he wrote of Adam's fall in the
Ninth Book of *Paradise Lost,*

> So rose the Danite strong,
> Herculean Samson from the harlot lap
> Of Philistean Dalilah, and waked
> Shorn of his strength, they desolate and bare
> Of all their virtue.[2]

In the tragedy itself he is concerned with the fallen Samson's recovery of God's lost favor. The process involves his punishment and repentance, and the facing of new trials with a firmness won of experience and faith. It involves also a reward in the consciousness of God's
having again accepted him as a worthy instrument of his purposes.

The trial itself is, I believe, the real center of the inward action, pro-
viding the play with such vital dramatic conflict as it exhibits. The
Chorus and Manoa continually suggest distrust and compromise. They
imply, in their attempted consolation, that Samson has been deceived
in his belief that he once enjoyed God's special favor and was his
chosen vessel. His marriages were not, as he had supposed, of a divine
suggestion. God's dealings in sending the angel of his birth and apparently electing him as the champion of Israel, only to desert and
leave him impotent, are unintelligible, if not unjust, for all has been
turned to the glory of the Philistines. Against this Samson opposes, on
the whole, the attitude of faith. He resists the suggestion that God was
not really with him in the past. He reiterates the cry that nothing of
all his evils has befallen him but justly. He meets the challenge of
Manoa's

> Yet Israel still serves with all his tribes,

with the rejoinder that it is they themselves who through their own
weakness have neglected God's proposed deliverance. For himself, he
knows that he has forfeited all hope, but he remains unshaken in the
belief that God will not

> Connive, or linger, thus provoked,
> But will arise, and his great name assert.

Throughout the dialogue there are marked similarities to the Book
of Job. Manoa and the Chorus have a function analogous to that of the

[2] Lines 1059-1062.

friends who sharpen Job's agony by their mistaken comfort. Samson's resistance of the attempt to shake the convictions of his innermost experience has its counterpart in Job's passionate denial of the imputation of unrighteousness. There is, of course, a formal contrast between the two, in that Samson, unlike Job, is afflicted by a sense of sin, but both are loyal to truth and both maintain their positions against the apparent facts. Both, finally, are rewarded for their consistency by a manifestation of God's approval. With Job it is the voice out of a whirlwind, with Samson the renewal of "rousing motions" of innermost impulse, which have stirred and guided him to great deeds before his fall.

Of these motives there is in the Scriptural account of Samson not the slightest hint. The hero of the Hebrew chronicle is a naïve and semi-humorous märchen figure, whose sluggish intellect is far removed from any capability of spiritual conflict. Milton preserves the traits of his impulsiveness of temper and his original simplicity of spirit, but endows him, after his disillusionment, with extraordinary force of mind and with penetrating insight. The infusion into this mighty champion of old, of the complex emotions of the maturest and most profound creation of Hebrew thought, is the last masterful stroke of Milton's genius. For it, he had, to my knowledge, no precedent in literary tradition.

But if Milton is indebted to Job for the most essential elements in his conception of Samson's character, it is to his own constructive imagination, working within the artistic forms provided by occidental drama, that he owes the development of his theme. In the Book of Job there is little outward action and no clear progression. In *Samson* there are both. The framework of the plot is that of a Greek play. It is simple even to meagerness. Samson is consoled by the Chorus, worried by Dalilah, insulted by Harapha, summoned before the Philistines by an officer. Old Manoa is busy meanwhile with misguided plans for his release, the moment of his success ironically coinciding with that of Samson's death. A messenger relates the catastrophe. The Chorus sings of Samson's fate and triumph.

Within this formal action the spiritual movement is richer than one at first observes. At the opening Samson is a spectacle of tragic misery and debasement. Out of his intense depression there rises higher and higher the note of active pain. At first his utterance concerns chiefly his physical and outward state:

> O loss of sight, of thee I most complain!
> Blind among enemies! O worse than chains,
> Dungeon or beggery, or decrepit age!

The first chorus, unheard by the protagonist, echoes and interprets his lament, with emphasis on the contrast between what once he was, is now. In the ensuing dialogue Samson's attention is diverted from his present wretchedness to its causes and significance. The memory of his fault is more bitter than the punishment wherewith it has been visited.

> Ye see, O friends,
> How many evils have enclosed me round;
> Yet that which once was the worst now least afflicts me,
> Blindness, for had I sight, confused with shame,
> How could I once look up, or heave the head,
> Who, like a foolish pilot, have shipwracked
> My vessel trusted to me from above.

The sight of Manoa wakes "another inward grief," and his words are as a goad to Samson's bitter remembrance. His proposal to treat with the Philistine lords serves only to reveal his son's indifference to his outward fate. The scene culminates in a spiritual outburst, expressive no longer of the hero's physical misery and obvious disgrace,

> Ensnared, assaulted, overcome, led bound,
> Thy foes' derision, captive, poor, and blind,

but of the inner agony of soul which springs from full contemplation of his sins, "and sense of Heaven's desertion." The opening words of the passage clearly indicate the forward movement:

> Oh, that torment should not be confined
> To the body's wounds and sores,
> With maladies innumerable
> In heart, head, breast, and reins,
> But must secret passage find
> To the inmost mind,
> There exercise all his fierce accidents,
> And on her purest spirits prey,
> As on entrails, joints, and limbs,
> With answerable pains, but more intense,
> Though void of corporal sense! [3]

---

[3] Lines 606-616.

The conclusion is one of unrelieved despair and marks the darkest moment of Samson's suffering, corresponding precisely to Adam's remorseful misery as he meditates upon his sin:

> Hopeless are all my evils, all remediless.
> This one prayer yet remains, might I be heard,
> No long petition—speedy death,
> The close of all my miseries and the balm.

Henceforth we have recovery. By confronting his own guilt without evasion, and by resisting the temptation to doubt God's ways are just, or to fear for the ultimate triumph of his cause, Samson has won the right to be put to proof a second time. His firmness is subjected first to the insidious approaches of Dalilah, whose visit, however doubtfully motivated in itself, is essential to the idea of the drama. Her plea is specious, but Samson remains unmoved, the significance of his victory being pointed out in the choric comment,

> Yet beauty, though injurious, hath strange power,
> After offence returning, to regain
> Love once possessed, nor can be easily
> Repulsed, without much inward passion felt
> And secret sting of amorous remorse.

He next confronts physical force in the person of Harapha, who collapses, like all brute menace, before the champion's indifference to fear, and the chorus, participating for the moment in Samson's strength, sings the great ode,

> O how comely it is, and how reviving,
> When God into the hands of their deliverer
> Puts invincible might,
> To quell the mighty of the earth, the oppressor,
> The brute and boistrous force of violent men.[4]

They are, of course, like Samson himself, still blind to what is to come, and they go on to sing of patience as the final crown of saints.

The coming of the officer creates a problem. Samson's refusal, at first, to do his bidding illustrates his uncompromising allegiance to the God of his fathers and his contempt of personal safety. The Chorus suggests the easier way of yielding, pointing out the fact that he has already served the Philistines (with the old implication that he cannot regard himself as a being set apart). Their reasoning is met with a

[4] Lines 1267 ff.

clear distinction between compromise in things indifferent and the surrender of a point of conscience. Then, as if in answer to this final proof of Samson's single devotedness to God's service, comes again the inner prompting, "disposing to something extraordinary my thoughts." He obeys it unhesitatingly and goes forth under divine guidance as of old. He has, in a sense, regained his own lost Paradise, and in his story Milton, by vindicating the power of a free but erring will to maintain itself in obedience and be restored to grace, has again asserted eternal Providence and justified the ways of God to man.

The fact that Samson is an Old Testament figure and achieves his triumph before the time of the Redeemer shows the true place of Christ in Milton's system. The blood of his sacrifice is plainly no necessary instrument of salvation; even his example may be dispensed with by those who enjoy a direct and special relation with the Divine. Yet the Hebrews did have Christ in prophecy, and for the men of later time he is the way. By his present example the path is open, not for chosen heroes alone, but for all, to

> love with fear the only God, to walk
> As in his presence, ever to observe
> His providence, and on him sole depend,
> Merciful over all his works, with good
> Still overcoming evil, and by small
> Accomplishing great things—by things deemed weak
> Subverting worldly-strong, and worldly-wise
> By simply meek;[5]

Such is Milton's final teaching and the ethical goal of his poetic art. The desire expressed in the introduction to Book IX of *Paradise Lost* to sing "the better fortitude of patience and heroic martyrdom" is fulfilled by the portrayal of a divine pattern in *Paradise Regained*. *Samson Agonistes* is its nearest possible fulfillment in the life of mortal man. To embody it more completely by representing the humbler trials and victories of daily life would have been incompatible with the tradition of Milton's literary allegiance—incompatible, too, with the memory of the heroic struggle in which he himself had been engaged.

Of this experience and this struggle I have as yet said nothing. How deeply it enters into the bone and sinew of *Samson Agonistes* no one can doubt. That Milton felt the parallel between his own situation and that of Samson and that he in some way identified himself with

[5] *P. L.,* XII. 562-569.

his hero is obvious and has been emphasized by the biographers. I have myself elsewhere pointed out that in making Samson wrestle with despair, Milton was championing his own faith assaulted by inward murmuring and challenged by the apparent failure of his cause.[6] It remains to enquire as to the extent and nature of this personal identification and to analyze more exactly the psychological reactions, conscious and unconscious, which are implied in the composition of the play.

Let us recognize at once that *Samson Agonistes* is a work of art and not a disguised autobiography. To a reader unacquainted with Milton's life the poem would seem as monumentally independent as *Prometheus Bound*. It deserves to be so judged and would, perhaps, stand higher as a masterpiece of art if it had been less often used as an illustration of Milton's personal life and temper. It should not, however, suffer from interpretation in the light of the poet's characteristic moods and thoughts, if we clearly recognize the conditions of their operation in his creative work. His most intimate emotions are invariably sublimated by the imagination and so far depersonalized. The process enables him to project himself with sympathy into characters and situations which have only a partial analogy with his own. So it is with his representations of Comus, or of Satan and Adam in *Paradise Lost*. In other cases, as in those of Dalilah, Eve, or Mammon he is capable, within a limited range, of being as objective as any artist of essentially romantic temper.

In the representation of Samson, Milton has undoubtedly put more of himself than in any other of his imaginative creations. The sense of power and dignity, the "plain heroic magnitude of mind," the will toward championship are Milton. So too is the noble self-pity, expressed in the consciousness of deprivation in the loss of sight ("The sun to me is dark, and silent as the moon"), and the feeling of physical helplessness ("In power of others, never in my own"). But all this is heightened and idealized for purposes of art. The tragic gloom and flat despair of Samson, the wretchedness of pain, the distaste of life, are the embodiments of an aesthetic mood which owes quite as much to literature as to personal experience. As a matter of fact the impression left by such direct biographical records as we have of Milton in old age is quite the reverse of this, suggesting the persistence in him to the end of a temper unspoiled by tribulation. The "cheerful godliness" of

---

[6] "The Temptation Motive in Milton," *Studies in Philology*, XV (1918), pp. 176-94.

Wordsworth's sonnet appears to be an entirely appropriate description of the poet's habitual outward mood in the last years of his life.

With regard to his blindness it is worth noting that the most poignant allusions to it were written longest after the event itself. At the actual moment of the catastrophe Milton was silent. His poetical occupation in the immediately succeeding years was the translation of Psalms, a literary and religious discipline. In 1654 he gives expression in prose, not to his sense of irrecoverable loss, but to the consciousness of spiritual compensation in "an interior illumination more precious and more pure." [7] In 1655, on the third anniversary of his loss of sight, he allows himself to consider how his "light is spent ere half his days," and to give voice to the pathos of his condition, only, however, as a preparation for the expression of acquiescence and of the consolations which come from the sense of having sacrificed himself in a noble cause. The utterances in *Paradise Lost* are touched with a deeper pathos, but it is first in *Samson,* where they are no longer directly personal, that they become a tragic cry:

> Dark, dark, dark, amid the blaze of noon,
> Irrecoverably dark, total eclipse,
> Without all hope of day.

A similar account might be given of the poet's antifeminism. It is entirely absent from the sonnets which belong to the days of his estrangement from Mary Powell. Indeed the two poems written at that time, *To a Virtuous Young Lady* and *To the Lady Margaret Ley,* are sincere though sober tributes to female virtue. The general indictment of the sex begins with Adam's words to Eve in Book X of *Paradise Lost* and reaches a strain of unrelieved bitterness in *Samson Agonistes.*

Such are the facts, as we read them in the chronological consideration of Milton's works. One cannot fail to be struck by the analogy which exists between the processes of the poet's expression of certain phases of his inmost experience in this last epoch of his literary life and his youthful development. The position of *Samson Agonistes* in its relation to the complex of emotions and ideas which centered in the poet's blindness is singularly like that of *Comus* with reference to the conflict of sensuous and ideal impulses in his adolescence. Each represents the culmination of a train of introspective thoughts which may easily be conceived to have been disturbing to Milton's mental equilibrium. In

---

[7] [Milton,] *Defensio Secunda, Prose Works* (Bohn) [1846], I, 239.

each work he appears to achieve for the first time a full expression of these emotions, and in achieving it to obtain a spiritual mastery of them. The result is one which is always, perhaps, in some degree present in the intenser activity of the creative imagination, and it has received general recognition from the critics and philosophers of literature. The most luminous statement is the following by Croce in his *Aesthetic*.[8] "By elaborating his impressions, man frees himself from them. By objectifying them, he removes them from him and makes himself their superior. The liberating and purifying function of art is another aspect and another formula of its character as activity. Activity is the deliverer, just because it drives away passivity. This also explains why it is usual to attribute to artists both the maximum of sensibility and the maximum of insensibility or Olympian serenity. The two characters are compatible, for they do not refer to the same object. The sensibility or passion relates to the rich material which the artist absorbs into his psychic organism, the insensibility or serenity to the form with which he subdues and dominates the tumult of sensations and passions."

It is scarcely possible to determine the degree to which Milton, in recreating and transforming emotions which in their rawer form made inroads upon his carefully cherished serenity, experienced a similar deliverance. Some light may be gained, however, by a consideration of certain neglected aspects of the play itself, the indications, namely, which the poet has given of what he himself thought of its function as a work of art. These indications refer mainly, to be sure, to what he looked for in its effect upon the reader or spectator, but they are not without application to the artist as well, and it seems to me quite clear that Milton must have been guided in his interpretation of the power of tragedy to effect spiritual benefits upon others by what he had himself experienced in creating it.

The question centers in his understanding of the formula for tragedy and its purgative effect as given in the famous Aristotelian definition. The importance of this formula in Milton's thought and the degree to which he must have been conscious of it in constructing his drama are suggested by the fact that he quotes it in Latin on his title page and devotes the first part of his prose preface to its elaboration. His opening statement is as follows: "Tragedy as it was anciently composed hath been ever held the gravest, moralest, and most profitable of all other

---

[8] Chapter 2. Douglas Ainsley's translation, 1922.

poems; therefore said by Aristotle to be of power by raising pity and fear, or terror, to purge the mind of those and such like passions, that is to temper and reduce them to just measure with a kind of delight, stirred up by seeing those passions well imitated." In considering the application of this principle to *Samson Agonistes* we must observe, first of all, that, by representing a clearly marked triumph of the human will over its own weakness, and by the substitution of Providence for blind fate as the power which overrules the action, the play provides material for a different understanding of catharsis from that contemplated by Aristotle, an understanding which falls in with the first part of Milton's description—that tragedy is the gravest, moralest, and most profitable of poetic forms—rather than with the last—that it transforms painful emotions into pleasurable. On a superficial view we might, indeed, be tempted to regard the purgation, as Milton actually worked it out, as a purely ethical and religious process, the result of a consciously didactic purpose by which our faith is strengthened and our sympathy with Samson's pain swallowed up in our exultation in his triumph. It is the function of Manoa's last speech and of the final chorus to emphasize this motive:

> Come, come, no time for lamentation now,
> Nor much more cause; Samson hath quit himself
> Like Samson, and heroicly hath finished
> A life Heroic. . . .
> With God not parted from him as was feared,
> But favouring and assisting to the end.
>
> .  .  .  .  .  .  .  .  .
>
> All is best, though we oft doubt,
> What the unsearchable dispose
> Of highest wisdom brings about
> And ever best found in the close.

To some critics[9] these quotations have seemed an adequate formula for the poem as a whole, and a mark of the failure of *Samson Agonistes* to embody the genuinely tragic motive of the unsuccessful struggle of man with fate. Such a judgment is obvious and in part correct. It fails, however, to take account of the actuality of the tragic impression which the drama must leave upon every reader who comes to it unhampered by definitions and comparisons. The pain of the earlier scenes is some-

[9] See Paull F. Baum, *"Samson Agonistes* Again," *Publications of the Modern Language Association,* XXXVI (1921), 365 ff.

thing which cannot be so easily displaced. Sealed as it is with the hero's
death, it outlives all consolation, as the tragic suffering of Hamlet outlives the accomplishment of his purpose, the choric benediction of
Horatio, and the restoration of a wholesome commonwealth by Fortin-
bras. The pronouncement "All is best" is of scarcely more avail than
the identical formulae which bring Greek plays to their conclusion and
from which this one is derived. The consolation which is offered of
"what can quiet us in a death so noble" is not enough. Samson should
have gone on from one glad triumph to another and emerged un-
scathed. Outward circumstance, the treacheries of others, and his own
conspiring fault have brought him low, and have constrained him to
wear, however gloriously, the crown of martyrdom. Here surely is tragedy enough. Though Providence is proclaimed, its ways are dark and
its face, at times, is hardly to be distinguished from the countenance of
Fate herself. The secret is that there remains an irreducible element in
the midst of Milton's faith—a sense as keen as Shakespeare's of the
reality of suffering which neither the assurance of God's special favors
to himself nor his resolute insistence on the final triumph of his right-
eousness can blot out. The antique strain in Milton's experience and
thought stands side by side with the Christian, and the two alternate
or combine in their domination, of his artistic moods. It is in vain that
he repudiates stoicism as a futile refuge and a false philosophy; he is
betrayed by the vehemence of his declarations against it, and he instinctively adopts its weapons.

These considerations prepare us to examine the operation in
*Samson Agonistes* of catharsis in its strict Aristotelian sense. Milton's
effort to demonstrate in his drama the truth of Aristotle's pronouncement is part and parcel of a thoroughgoing conscious classicism, which
extends far beyond such matters as the ordering of the incidents and
the employment of ancient devices like the messenger. It is shown in
a more philosophic and intrinsic way in the subtle turns which the
poet gives to the interpretation of his theme in order to bring it more
nearly into conformity with the spirit of ancient tragedy. Professor
Baum[10] counts it a major defect of *Samson Agonistes* that the hero's
tragic fault is undignified and sub-heroic. But observe the means which
Milton takes to dignify it. He associates it with the most dignified of
all tragic faults—rebellious pride. Intoxicated by success, Samson for-
gets to refer his victories to their source, and so becomes, in Milton's

[10] *Loc. cit.*

interpretation, an instance of classical hybris. Like Shakespeare's Mark
Antony he "struts to his destruction."

> Fearless of danger, like a petty God,
> I walked about, admired of all, and dreaded
> On hostile ground, none daring my assault.
> Then swollen with pride, into the snare I fell
> Of fair fallacious looks, venerial trains.[11]

This is somewhat forced, one must confess, and Milton appears to be
aware of it. Witness the shading he is compelled to give to the idea in
the following:

> But I
> God's counsel have not kept, his holy secret
> Presumptiously have published, impiously,
> *Weakly at least and shamefully*—a sin
> That Gentiles in their parables condemn
> To their Abyss and horrid pains confined.[12]

The cloak of Prometheus and Tantalus evidently refuses to fit the less
majestic Hebrew Titan. The conception of hybris and Ate applies more
perfectly to the Philistines and is accordingly invoked in the triumphant semi-chorus beginning in line 1669:

> While their hearts were jocund and sublime,
> Drunk with idolatry, drunk with wine
> And fat regorged of bulls and goats,
> Chaunting their idol, and preferring
> Before our Living Dread, who dwells
> In Silo, his bright sanctuary,
> Among them he a spirit of phrenzy sent,
> Who hurt their minds,
> And urged them on with mad desire
> To call in haste for their destroyer.
> They, only set on sport and play,
> Unweetingly importuned
> Their own destruction to come speedy upon them.
> So fond are mortal men,
> Fallen into wrath divine,
> As their own ruin on themselves to invite,
> Insensate left, or to sense reprobate,
> And with blindness internal struck.

[11] Lines 529-533.
[12] Lines 496-501.

Both passages, however, are illustrative of the degree to which Milton had grasped the central motive of Greek tragedy and the pains he was at to bring his own material under the ethical, religious, and artistic formulae afforded by it.

A more vital result of his assimilation of the point of view of his ancient models is to be found in the great chorus which follows Samson's deeper expression of despair, in lines 608-650. If anything in Milton or indeed in all modern literature deserves to be called a reproduction of antiquity it is this passage. It is as perfectly representative as Milton could have wished of "Aeschylus, Sophocles, Euripides, the three tragic poets unequalled yet by any, and the best rule to all who endeavor to write Tragedy," and it comes little short of their noblest choral odes in the grandeur and intensity of its tragic feeling. In the majestic rhythms of the opening the Chorus sings of the vanity of consolation in the ears of the afficted and expostulates with Providence in its uneven course with men. Thoroughly Greek and as thoroughly Miltonic is the centering of attention on the woes, not of the common rout of men who grow up and perish like the summer fly, but on those of heroic mould, "with gifts and graces eminently adorned." The ensuing lines embody the idea of the excess of evil which rains down on the head of the tragic hero according to Aristotle's description in the *Poetics:*

> Nor only dost degrade them, or remit
> To life obscured, which were a fair dismission,
> But throw'st them lower than thou didst exalt them high—
> Unseemly falls in human eye,
> Too grievous for the trespass or omission;
> Oft leav'st them to the hostile sword
> Of heathen and profane, their carcasses
> To dogs and fowls a prey, or else captived,
> Or to the unjust tribunals, under change of times,
> And condemnation of the ungrateful multitude.
> If these they escape, perhaps in poverty
> With sickness and disease thou bow'st them down,
> Painful diseases and deformed,
> In crude old age;
> Though not disordinate, yet causeless suffering
> The punishment of dissolute days. In fine,
> Just or unjust alike seem miserable,
> For oft alike both come to evil end.

The personal note here is too distinct to be mistaken. "Unjust tri-
bunals under change of times," "their carcasses to dogs and fowls a
prey" are certainly echoes of the Restoration, with its brutal trials of
men like Henry Vane, and the indignities to which the bodies of Crom-
well and Ireton were subjected. The parallel and not less wretched
fate of poverty and disease is Milton's own. He goes so far as almost to
specify the rheumatic ills from which we know him to have suffered—
"painful diseases and deformed"—with the bitter reflection that these
afflictions, justly the fruit of dissipation, may come also to those who,
like himself, have lived in temperance. Nowhere else in his works, not
even in the laments of Adam, does Milton permit himself to indulge
in so unrelieved an expression of pagan sentiment. He does so under
the shield of dramatic objectivity, yet none of his words spring from
deeper sources in his consciousness. Here momentarily he faces the
world with no other arms than those of pure humanity, giving utterance to a view of life directly opposed to that to which he had subdued
his thinking as a whole.

It is in such a mood as this and in such an utterance that Milton
must, if ever, have felt, in his own emotional experience, the reality of
the Aristotelian catharisis, and the need of it. The question of the means
whereby affliction may be soothed is one which had always interested
him, and his works contain numerous suggestive utterances on the subject. It is prominent in the discussion of the case of Samson. Thus, con-
templating, at this point, his hero's misery, he makes the Chorus tell
how useless for the sufferer in his pangs are those wise consolations of
philosophy, "writ with studied argument, lenient of grief and anxious
thought." It is only, they affirm, by "secret refreshings from above" that
the afflicted wretch can be restored. But such refreshings are obviously
not always to be commanded. To prepare for their benign influence
the mind must first be emptied of its pent-up bitterness, and for such a
process tragedy, in the Aristotelian conception, supplies the means. So,
one would suppose, might Milton have thought and felt. And if such
was his experience it is not surprising that he should have dwelt with
such insistence on the rationale of the process in his prose preface.

His initial statement I have already quoted. Pity, fear, and like
passions, it implies, are, in their raw state, dangerous and painful.
Objectively represented, they are tempered and reduced to just measure
by a kind of delight. "Nor is Nature," adds Milton, "wanting in her
own effects to make good his assertion; for so, in Physic, things of

melancholic hue and quality are used against melancholy, sour against
sour, salt to remove salt humours." This passage has often been cited
with approval by classical scholars as expressing the soundest modern
interpretation of the dark oracle of Aristotle's pronouncement, and
there has been discussion of Milton's priority in employing the med-
ical analogy. No one, I think, has called attention to his application of
this conception to the analysis of Samson's spiritual ills in an outstand-
ing passage in the play itself. The hero has just expressed his indifference to the efforts proposed in his behalf and his expectation of an
early death. Manoa replies:

> Believe not these suggestions, which proceed
> From anguish of the mind, and humours black
> That mingle with thy fancy.[13]

There follows the great lyric outburst of Samson's spiritual woe, which
must now be given at greater length.

> O that torment should not be confined
> To the body's wounds and sores,
> With maladies innumerable
> In heart, head, breast, and reins;
> But must secret passage find
> To the inmost mind,
> There exercise all his fierce accidents,
> And on her purest spirits prey,
> As on entrails, joints and limbs,
> With answerable pains, but more intense,
> Though void of corporal sense!
> My griefs not only pain me
> As a lingering disease,
> But, finding no redress, ferment and rage;
> Nor less than wounds immedicable
> Rankle, and fester, and gangrene,
> To black mortification.
> Thoughts, my tormentors, armed with deadly stings,
> Mangle my apprehensive tenderest parts,
> Exasperate, exulcerate, and raise
> Dire inflammation, which no cooling herb
> Or medicinal liquor can assuage,
> Nor breath of vernal air from snowy Alp.
> Sleep hath forsook and given me o'er

[13] Lines 599-601.

To death's benumbing opium as my only cure;
Thence faintings, swoonings of despair,
And sense of Heaven's desertion.

The idea which Milton here develops with somewhat shocking ex-
plicitness is obviously the same as that which underlies his conception
of catharsis—the idea, namely, that the passions operate in precisely
the manner of bodily poisons, which, when they find no outlet, rage
destructively within. Samson is given over to pity and fear, and there
is no apparent prospect of relief, no cooling herb or medicinal liquor
to purify the "black mortification" of his thoughts. It is quite clear,
then, that Milton intends to suggest a kind of Aristotelian diagnosis of
Samson's tragic state, parallel to the more obvious religious interpretation which I have previously expounded. But if he partly identified
himself with his hero, then such a diagnosis would serve also to that
extent to describe his own. As, however, he draws a sharp distinction
on the religious side between Samson's spiritual darkness and his own
illumination by an inner light, so here he must have been conscious of
a difference in the manner of their deliverance from the morbid in-
trospection to which they are equally subject. The intensity of Samson's pain lasts only so long as he remains inactive. His lyric elaboration of his inward woe is immediately followed by the unexpected
visits of his foes. His attention is thus distracted from his suffering to
a series of situations which confront him and he finally loses himself
in glorious though disastrous action.

For Milton, in the impotence of his situation after the Restoration,
there can be no such deliverance. He is enrolled perforce among those
"whom patience finally must crown." But he has in his possession a
recourse without which the way of patience is at times too hard. The
purgation which the untutored champion of Israel must find in deeds
is available to the man of culture through the activity of the mind and
spirit. It offers itself to Milton in a dual form, corresponding to his
twofold inheritance from the Reformation and the Renaissance. As
the play draws to an end the two motives are subtly balanced and
as nearly reconciled as, perhaps, it is within the power of human
skill to reconcile them. The champion's final deed and the triumph
of God's uncontrollable intent promote in us a sense of exultation
and confirm our faith, but the greatness of his suffering and the
pathos of his death produce a different effect, making possible the
serene dismission of the close:

> His servants he, with new acquist
> Of true experience from this great event,
> With peace and consolation hath dismissed
> And calm of mind, all passion spent.

It is characteristic of the critical self-consciousness which Milton carries with him even in his moments of highest creative inspiration and suggestive also of the vital uses to which he turned aesthetic as well as religious doctrine that the last word of all should be an almost explicit reference to the tragic formula which he had derived from the authority of "the master of those who know."

# Milton's Debt to Greek Tragedy in
# *Samson Agonistes:* The Problem of Spirit

## *by William Riley Parker*

No less a scholar than Sir Richard Jebb has given his opinion that
'*Samson Agonistes* may fairly be called classical both in language and
in structure.' [1] His essay on '*Samson Agonistes* and the Hellenic Drama'
(read before the British Academy several years after his death) not
only indicates some of the analogies already examined in the present
study, but also offers a slightly new answer to Dr. Johnson's criticism of the play's 'middle.' It is ironic, however—in a way which Jebb
would have appreciated—that while thus minimizing the influence of
Johnson as a critic of *Samson,* Jebb himself gave expression to a
generalization which has ever since—thanks to his great prestige as
a scholar—awed a number of commentators into uncritical acceptance
or very respectful protest. The matter is of sufficient importance to
be considered in detail. Jebb declares:

> A more interesting inquiry than any regarding the form of the *Samson
> Agonistes* is that regarding its spirit. Granting it to be in diction and in
> structure representative of that Greek drama which was its model, how
> far, we ask, is it animated by the spirit, by the dominant idea, of its
> original? This point appears to have been too little considered by the
> critics of Milton's great poem.[2]

With these preliminary remarks, we must agree. Jebb is quite correct
in saying that the question of 'spirit' had been too little considered,
and I feel, therefore, that no apologies are necessary for the space which
I shall devote to it here. Imitating the form of classical tragedy is one

---

[1] *Proceedings of the British Academy,* iii (London: 1907-8), 341.
[2] *Ibid.,* p. 343.

thing, but capturing the spirit of classical tragedy is another and a greater thing. How far has Milton succeeded? Jebb would contend that he has failed. He devotes a paragraph to Matthew Arnold's definitions of 'Hebraism' and 'Hellenism,' [3] and then proceeds to the dangerous but fascinating business of classifying Milton.

> Milton's mind was, in the literal and proper sense, Hebraic. . . . When a man with this bent of thought selected as the subject for a poem an episode of Hebrew history, the treatment of the subject was sure to be genuinely Hebraic. . . . Samson is the champion of the Israelites against the Philistines. Jehovah is the God of the Israelites; Dagon is the protecting deity of the Philistines. Samson, through disloyalty to himself, has been permitted to fall into the hands of the idolaters; and Israel shares in his humiliation. Yet, even in this abasement, Samson is confident that the Lord of Hosts will finally assert His own majesty against the idol. This confidence is justified: the honour of the true God and of His chosen people are vindicated by the catastrophe which punishes the weakness, as it closes the penance, of His individual minister. This is the issue of the drama—Jehovah has prevailed over Dagon; Israel is avenged on Philistia.[4]

This summing up of the play we shall later examine. But let us do justice to his argument:

> The first characteristic of Hellenic tragedy in the hands of its greatest masters was an ideal grandeur of agony depending on a real grandeur of contrast. The contrast was between man and fate. The subject of Greek tragedy in all its forms, in all the fables over which it ranged, was the conflict between free will and destiny, between an absolute inward liberty and an inexorable external necessity. . . . The question so often asked, what is the source of imaginative pleasure in tragedy? is thus answered by Hellenic tragedy: it is the sense, on the one hand, of the heroic in man; on the other hand, of a superhuman controlling power . . . Hellenism contrasts man with fate. Hebraism contrasts God and His servants with idols and their servants.[5]

In order to illustrate this point, Jebb offers a comparison of Samson with Herakles, the point of which he expresses as follows:

---

[3] I avoid any discussion of Arnold's terms, because Jebb announces his intention of using them 'in a narrower and stricter acceptation.' Perhaps this is the place, however, to record my impression that Jebb did not keep his promise—that the labels tricked him, as they have tricked many a lesser man. Literary labels constitute one of the scholar's most dangerous friends.

[4] *Op. cit.*, pp. 343-44.

[5] *Op. cit.*, pp. 344-45.

The central idea of Samson's history, and, in harmony with that history, the central idea of Milton's poem, is the idea of a national champion, first victorious, then abased, then finally triumphant in a national cause. The feeling uppermost in Samson's mind is this—that the strength entrusted to him for the honour of God and of Israel has, through his own weakness, been betrayed and crushed; and that the great cause which he was commissioned to uphold has thereby been dishonoured. . . . The central idea of the story of Herakles is that of a champion of the whole human race, persecuted throughout his mortal life by a cruel destiny. . . . Samson in his death triumphs over the Philistines; Herakles in his last agony is the victim of fate.[6]

Having thus disposed of the matter, Jebb concludes his criticism of the spirit of Milton's *Samson* with a positive pronouncement: 'The *Samson Agonistes* is a great poem; it is also a noble drama. . . . But neither as poem nor as drama is it Hellenic.' [7]

Now before we look any further into the problem, this much must be made plain: whether Jebb be right or wrong, his entire criticism turns upon one point which must be thoroughly understood. He defines spirit as 'the dominant idea.' Jebb, I feel confident, would have readily admitted this qualification; his paper is, after all, comparatively brief, and his dogmatism is not without reasonable justification in the circumstances. But it has borne strange fruit.[8]

---

[6] *Ibid.,* p. 346.

[7] *Ibid.,* p. 348. Compare the milder statement in his *Growth and Influence of Classical Greek Poetry* (London: The Macmillan Co., 1893), pp. 274-75.

[8] Elbert N. S. Thompson allowed this problem to lead him into contradictions. '*Samson Agonistes* is an even closer copy than the epic of a classic pattern,' he tells us, 'but its spirit and content are *purely Hebraic.*' Then—in his very next sentence: 'In regard to this play the problem would be to determine how much the thought and spirit of the Attic playwrights *modified* Milton's Hebraism.' *Essays on Milton* (New Haven: Yale University Press, 1914), p. 148 (my italics). Paull Franklin Baum, after expressing his general agreement with Jebb, vigorously criticized the 'theme' of *S. A.*—including under this term the protagonist's character, the play's ending, the omission of Fate, and the belief in a just God, all of which he declared were un-Hellenic. *Publications of the Modern Language Association,* XXXVI (1921), 365-71. It is not necessary to multiply these instances of Jebb's 'influence.' W. C. Curry has said that *S. A.* has 'no relation with Greek tragedy in either spirit or structure, except for a superficial resemblance in form.' *Sewanee Review,* July, 1924, p. 350. Elmer Edgar Stoll has insisted on the Hebraism of *Samson* in order to counteract the recent view 'that Milton was not so much a Puritan as a humanist, a son of the Renaissance and of the classical world.' *S. A.,* declares Professor Stoll, is the most Puritan of all the major poems. Its 'central situation . . . is that of temptation. What could be more Puritan? What less Greek? . . . It is not a question of temperance, moderation, or the golden mean at all.' *Poets' and Playwrights* (Minneapolis: University of Minnesota Press, 1930), pp. 226, 232-33.

To be sure, mild exception was taken to his views by John Bailey. While admitting that Milton's 'angry sternness of judgment' and 'assured faith in divine deliverance' are 'rather Hebrew than Greek,' [9] he nevertheless—with 'a sense of great temerity'—suggests that Jebb was

> apt to feel small differences . . . too much and broad resemblances too little. To the shepherd all his sheep differ from each other: the danger for him is to forget, what the ignorant stranger sees, that they are also all very much alike. So Jebb is no doubt perfectly right in the distinction he makes: but he is surely blinded by his own knowledge when he argues from it that *Samson Agonistes* 'is a great poem and a noble drama; but neither as poem nor as drama is it Hellenic.' Of that question comparative ignorance is perhaps a better judge. For it can still see that the broad division which separates the world's drama into two kinds is a real thing, and that Milton's drama belongs in spite of differences unquestionably to the Greek kind and not to the other, both by its method and by its spirit.[10]

The analogy of the shepherd and his sheep is illuminating and delightful; but I venture to suggest that in considering this problem of spirit, we must find a clearer and a more comprehensive approach. The problem is not to be solved by labelling certain elements in the *Samson* 'Hebraic' or 'Puritan.' Of course there are 'Hebraic' and 'Puritan' features in Milton—but there are also 'Hebraic' and 'Puritan' features in Aeschylus.[11] Are we to say, therefore, that the tragedies of Aeschylus have not the 'Greek spirit'? Obviously this matter of 'spirit' is a broader, more inclusive thing than certain critics would have us believe. We cannot pin it down to a specific belief in fate; we cannot, I submit, pin it down to a specific belief at all. Aeschylus, Sophocles, and Euripides differed radically in their various opinions (though we are still, as it happens, quarrelling over the nature of those opinions!). Who, then, was 'Greek' and who was not? Would *Samson Agonistes* be truly Hellenic if the blind hero, in pulling down the temple, had killed no one but himself? Would it have satisfied modern critics if the final chorus had sung of a cruel and remorseless God? Is the

---

[9] *Milton* (London: Oxford University Press, 1915), p. 219.

[10] *Ibid.*, pp. 242-43.

[11] Jebb himself makes this point. *Growth and Influence of Classical Greek Poetry*, p. 215. See also [Arthur E. Haigh, *The Tragic Drama of the Greeks* (Oxford: The Clarendon Press, 1925), pp. 91-2, 104; W. H. Smyth, Loeb *Aeschylus* (1922-26), vol. 1, xxiv.]

*Eumenides* Greek? Is the *Oedipus Coloneus*? What shall we say of the *Philoctetes,* the two *Iphigeneia's*—all those plays, in fact, which have an almost happy ending? In the last analysis, are not most of our measuring rods hopelessly inadequate? Do we not insult the genius, the artistic sympathy of John Milton when we attempt to apply them to his work?

I shall not leave unchallenged some of the points made by Jebb and others; these critics are often guilty of misplacing emphasis; but for the moment I should like to consider the whole problem in a larger sense than they have chosen to adopt. What may we reasonably call the 'spirit' of Attic tragedy?

The term, I believe, may justifiably be used in two distinct senses, both of them broad. It may be used to denote the tone or temper resulting from certain animating or controlling *artistic* principles, conscious or unconscious, which find expression in the work of the three great tragedians. Or, on the other hand, it may be used to denote the tone or temper resulting from certain dominant ideas, *other than artistic,* which find direct or indirect expression in the work of the three great tragedians. Perhaps finally the true Greek 'spirit' is a combination of these two tones; in a sense, I realize, they are inseparable. But for the sake of clarity let us distinguish between them here.

And the first tone—that resulting from artistic principles—need occupy us but a moment. Almost no one has been rash enough to suggest that *Samson Agonistes,* from this point of view, is other than 'Greek.' The bulk of the present study has been devoted to proving Milton's conformity to Attic standards of construction, handling of material, treatment of character, and so on. We have noticed his respect for the two classical principles which came most obviously under this category: symmetry and restraint. We have indicated his creative familiarity with the *Poetics* of Aristotle. And it has been sufficiently clear, I hope, that Milton's success in grasping this artistic spirit was the result, not of slavish imitation or of perfunctory obedience to rules, but of genuine re-creation of Greek tragedy—a re-creation made possible by genius working with complete sympathy for the principles which produced the originals. It is this conformity to the artistic creed of the Greeks which Sir Edmund Chambers has chiefly in mind when he praises the 'spirit' of *Samson.* He mentions, let us notice, the use of rhetoric and irony, the emphasis on serenity, and the management of the chorus.[12] Similarly, it is 'the symmetry, the subtle union of greatness and grace, the restraint and lucidity of the art'[13] which Verity seems to understand by 'spirit.' Did not Goethe use the term in this sense when he said: *Samson* 'has more of the antique spirit than any production of any other modern poet'?[14] These are all statements, of course, with which Jebb would gladly agree. Jebb was thinking of spirit in terms of 'dominant idea'—not of technique. Let us look, therefore, at the second of our two categories.

Here we are on ground made uncertain by the never-ending process of interpretation. We shall have to walk circumspectly, meeting 'Hebraic' temptations with as much 'Hellenic' restraint as we can muster; for in the case of both *Samson Agonistes* and the Attic tragedies we shall find commentators who will tell us exactly what opinions their authors held. Our task would be easier if these commentators could agree, but, unfortunately, we are confronted with a bewildering variety of interpretations. Aeschylus was apparently a Hebrew prophet disguised as an Athenian. Euripides was a misogynist, but also a feminist. And Milton, it seems, was a Puritan, a Hebrew, a Greek, and a Renaissance gentleman. It is needless to elaborate the point; anyone familiar with the body of Milton criticism or the many books which have been written on Attic tragedy can call to mind too many illustrations.

The key to this difficulty is the fact that we are dealing with dramatists, not with lyric poets; and no matter how strong the subjective element may seem to be, we must be very careful to distinguish between personal opinion and opinion dictated by dramatic necessity. I would not deny that 'Milton, who presents in his works an image both of himself and of his life, is openly subjective, and in *Samson Agonistes* obliquely autobiographical';[15] nevertheless, we shall do well to remember Milton's own warning:

> One is not to regard what the poet says, but what person in the play speaks, and what that person says; for different persons are introduced, sometimes good, sometimes bad; sometimes wise men, sometimes fools; and such words are put into their mouths, as it is most proper for them

[12] *S. A.* (ed. Chambers) (London: Blackie & Son, 1897), pp. 21-2. The spirit, he says, is 'marvellously caught.'
[13] *S. A.* (ed. Verity) (Cambridge: Pitt Press, 1892), p. li.
[14] *Conversations,* ii.
[15] E. H. Visiak, *Milton Agonistes* (London: Philpot, 1923), p. 99.

to speak; not such as the poet would speak, if he were to speak in his own person.[16]

This observation was made, significantly for us, about the Greek dramatists. Let us bear it in mind as we search for the ideas implicit in *Samson*.

There is another vital consideration which must be made very plain. We have seen that the 'spirit' of Greek tragedy is of two kinds —artistic and (for want of a better word) intellectual. Moreover, in defining these distinct yet closely related categories, we have spoken of certain tones which *result from* various principles or ideas expressed by the Greek tragedians. The 'spirit,' in other words, is the tone or temper *resulting from* idea—it is not the idea itself. The idea or the artistic principle is but the means to the end. The same spirit may, or may not, be produced by a quite different idea. But it is the spirit that matters. Perhaps, in the last analysis, spirit is something more even than a tone resulting from the expression of principles or ideas; there must also be the sympathetic breath of genius—the breath that gives life to a work of art. For as Verity verily says:

> A man might lay to heart all the canons of the *Poetics*, and in choice of subject, in construction of plot, in delineation of his characters, deviate never a hand's breadth from the principles of the ancients, and yet fail —as French tragedians for all their pains often failed, as the early Elizabethans habitually failed—to produce work in which should dwell the presence—the *vivida vis*—of true, living art.[17]

The 'indefinable something' which, according to Verity, makes *Samson Agonistes* truly Greek, I should want to call Milton's fine understanding of the tone, of the end, which the Attic dramatists attained by the expression of their various principles and beliefs. Milton was too great an artist to confuse means and end. He would not identify 'rules' with 'spirit.' And no more, I think, would he feel it necessary to identify the spiritual tone, the 'intellectual' impression left by Greek tragedy, with the specific ideas which, in their day, produced that impression.

This appears, on the face of it, to be an extremely simple point; but it is the crux of the whole argument. Failure to recognize such a simple point has led to many errors of inference. Thus, Jebb may be correct when he says that 'the first characteristic of Hellenic tragedy

---

[16] Milton, *First Defence Prose Works* (Bohn), 1846, I, 126.
[17] *S. A.* (ed. Verity), p. 1.

in the hands of its greatest masters was an ideal grandeur of agony depending on a real grandeur of contrast.' This is a pregnant summary of one aspect of the tone—a summary which Jebb's long acquaintance with the Attic masters enabled him to make. But in his very next sentence, Jebb's long acquaintance with the Attic masters leads him astray; to employ a trite metaphor, he is too conscious of the trees to see the woods. 'The contrast,' he continues, 'was between man and fate.' And because Greek tragedy partly achieved its tone through the expression of this idea, Milton's tragedy must do the same, or it is not Greek in spirit. Hellenic tragedy gives us, we are told, a 'sense, on the one hand, of the heroic in man; on the other hand, of a superhuman controlling power.' But Jebb does not inquire whether or not *Samson Agonistes* leaves us with these two impressions. Rather, he points out that Samson is not a victim of fate; *ergo,* Samson is not Greek. He identifies cause with effect, and, finding the former absent in Milton's poem, fails to look for the latter.[18]

Let us, therefore, in order to resolve the problem, ask the question: What are the general impressions, *other than aesthetic,* gained from a reading of the Attic dramas? For the moment we are not interested in themes or opinions or dominant ideas. What, instead, are the most noticeable characteristics of Greek tragedy? What is its tone?

First of all we must insist, with a fine disregard for the obvious, that Greek tragedy is almost uniformly *serious.* It is earnest to the point of gravity. With scarcely a trace of humor, it is dignified in a way which sets it apart from the tragedy of later times. This air of seriousness is enhanced by another important attribute: Greek tragedy is always *thoughtful*—thoughtful in a speculative, almost philosophical fashion. It is concerned with the great problems of human life; beneath its action is an unmistakable strain of reflection, of perpetual questioning. Then, too, it is *didactic;* here was art for life's sake. Though the great tragedians differed in methods, each of them regarded his work as an instrument of instruction. It is didactic, however, without being doctrinal. The desire to teach is seldom offensively evident. But if dogma is rarely flaunted, there is no doubting the *religious* spirit of the plays. Greek tragedy always retained traces of its origin. The speculation may be carried to dark and daring extremes, but the general tone of piety,

---

[18] In another place, however, Jebb writes of the 'spirit' of Attic tragedy under such subjects as material, didacticism, characterization, etc. *Growth and Influence,* pp. 185-91. If he had examined *S. A.* under these categories, his conclusions would probably have been quite different.

of reverence for the gods, never disappears. Tragedy, even when it pictures the undeserved misery of mortal life, remains an act of worship. Consequently, we may expect a last great quality of one, which is perhaps a blend, and a result, of all the others. Greek tragedy is essentially *sublime:* it always has elevation.

I do not assume for a moment that I have exhausted the problem of spirit by calling Attic drama serious, thoughtful, didactic, religious, and sublime. But these seem to me the major qualities of its tone, the qualities which most nearly apply to all of the extant plays, and which distinguish Attic tragedy from the tragedy of later times. Believing so, I deem it profitable to judge *Samson Agonistes* by these criteria.

Greek tragedy, as we have already pointed out, has little comic relief; but there may be some. . . .* Ignoring entirely the question of whether or not comic relief is proper to tragedy, we find humor so sparingly used by these dramatists that it does not seem to belong to their work, even when it serves an artistic purpose. It is so much the exception, in other words, that we seldom think of it in connection with the tone or spirit of Attic tragedy. This tone was made almost consistently serious, not only by the omission of humorous touches, but also by the selection of material from sacred legends, the preoccupation with solemn themes, and the dignified manner of treatment. One wonders, in reading Dryden or Johnson on comic relief, whether Shakespeare would have introduced a clown or a joking gravedigger into a drama of the Crucifixion.[19] We must not forget that ancient tragedy was religious—in source, in subject matter, and in spirit.

When we turn to Milton, we find complete agreement with this view, both in theory and practice.[20] In the preface to *Samson Agonistes,* after calling Greek tragedy 'the gravest' of poems, he writes of the modern 'Poets error of intermixing Comic stuff with Tragic sadness and gravity.' This 'error' he makes a deliberate effort to avoid. He will observe 'decorum' and 'discretion'; he has no wish 'corruptly to gratifie the people.' Let the 'judicious' see how well he has followed 'best example' in this. And indeed, it is apparent that Milton has made his play serious enough to meet the most rigorous of standards. Through it runs, as in the dramas of the Greeks, a sense of the gravity

* Here, as elsewhere in this essay, some material designed to illustrate or further define a point has been omitted—ED.

[19] The miracle plays do not constitute an answer to this question, for the Middle Ages were not so sensitive to the incongruous as was Shakespeare.

[20] Consider: 'the lofty grave Tragœdians.' *P. R.* iv, 261.

of human life.[21] The issues are profound; the manner is severe; the whole piece has an impressiveness which makes it truly Hellenic. As we have previously observed, the character of Samson has been altered to suit the tone; the prankish, rather fantastic fellow of the Biblical story never once puts in his appearance. Whatever his past may have been, Milton's protagonist is now terribly in earnest. And the plot itself is serious throughout. With the interest centered always on the fate of the hero, we are never allowed to forget the gravity of the situation. The *Samson* is, if anything, too solemn for the taste of modern readers.[22] But an Attic audience would not have found its sobriety monotonous. The relief which we have come to expect in the form of comic interludes, they found in the choral odes and the general tone of exaltation. The characteristic of Milton's poem which we might want to criticize, they would have considered a mark of artistic propriety. A tragedian does not laugh at trouble; his business is to capture it in words.

This serious tone of Greek tragedy was partly due, of course, to the other qualities we have mentioned. One expects seriousness, for example, in a drama which involves speculation, a drama which is essentially meditative. . . . Is Milton's drama 'Greek' in the respect we are discussing? It must be allowed that it is. The 'vein of profound and earnest thoughtfulness' is so great that one critic has called the play Milton's 'philosophical testament.' [23] There is what Haigh calls a 'pervading sense of the dark mystery of existence': 'God of our Fathers, what is man'? [24] There is tortured—not merely 'wistful'—'craving for knowledge concerning the ways of providence'; the Chorus says, 'Tax not divine disposal,' and Samson says, 'Appoint not heavenly disposition,' yet both the Chorus and Samson are continually driven to question. . . .

[21] 'The "crude apple that diverted Eve" was indeed a simple theme compared with the profound topics that are treated in *Samson Agonistes*.' Raleigh, *Milton* (London: Edward Arnold, 1900), p. 167.

[22] The reason is perhaps that we are more and more looking to drama for entertainment alone. Even F. L. Lucas protests that 'the theatre is not a hospital' (*Tragedy*, p. 31). We have completely dissociated tragedy and religion, and we are annoyed by the frankly didactic. We may accept G. B. Shaw's combination of philosophy and farce, but we usually refuse to countenance a serious attempt at instruction through drama. I have found students who simply could not stomach the unrelenting seriousness of *S. A.* Richard Garnett calls it 'an old man's poem'; 'there is much to repel, little to attract a young reader.' *Life of Milton*, p. 181.

[23] Denis Saurat, *Milton: Man and Thinker* (London: Jonathan Cape, 1925), p. 236.

[24] Haigh, p. 323; *S. A.* 667.

[Let us turn to] a third aspect of the Greek spirit—an attribute with which Milton had felt life-long sympathy. Attic drama is didactic in both tone and purpose. Aeschylus, Sophocles, and Euripides all had a high conception of the poet's duty, regarding tragedy as an instrument of instruction, and the tragic poet as a teacher of wisdom. They differed, however, in their interpretation of this duty. . . .

Indisputably, Milton agreed with Aeschylus that poets are teachers of men. The point scarcely calls for elaboration. His prose writings furnish many statements of this creed, but we really need look no further than the preface to *Samson Agonistes*. His opening remark draws attention to the position of tragedy as the 'moralest, and most profitable' of poems. His acceptance of the doctrine of katharsis is another evidence of his didactic purpose. And 'Philosophers,' we are told, 'frequently cite out of Tragic poets' in order to 'illustrate their discourse.' Indeed, *Samson Agonistes* is itself eloquent proof of Milton's desire to instruct. As certainly as in *Paradise Lost* there is present the intention of justifying God's ways to men; and as certainly as in everything Milton wrote there is present a more general tone of didacticism which, in weaker hands, would doubtless have proved fatal to art. It would be foolish to trace this characteristic to Milton's acquaintance with Greek tragedy. It may be 'Puritan' or 'Hebraic' in origin. But it is also Greek. . . . All Hellenic drama was essentially religious in spirit.[25] In origin an act of worship, it never completely lost its pious and reverent tone. Even Euripides, whose religious views have been the subject of much controversy, generally tended 'to inculcate respect and reverence for the established forms of belief.' . . .[26]

The most severe critic of *Samson Agonistes* would admit, I think, that Milton's drama also has a religious tone.[27] It is a point hardly requiring proof.[28] Let us notice, however, that the religious tone of the *Samson* is the result of convictions which do not tally, in all respects, with those of the Greeks. In spite of certain agreements, which will

[25] 'In all Greek tragedies, even those that are full of free thought, the whole permeating atmosphere is that of religion.' Gilbert Murray, *English Literature and the Classics* (Oxford: The Clarendon Press, 1912), p. 15.

[26] Haigh, p. 266.

[27] 'His drama is what Greek tragedies were, an act of worship. It could take its place quite naturally, as they did, as part of a great national religious festival performed on a holy day.' Bailey, *Milton*, p. 241.

[28] But consider Sheppard's interesting comment: 'On some aspects of theology and social theory, *Samson Agonistes* is more primitive and less religious than the "fabulous imaginations" of the Athenian poets. But the grim theology makes excellent drama.' *Aeschylus & Sophocles* (New York: Longmans & Green, 1927), p. 154.

be discussed in the next section, there is no denying that Milton did not express strictly Greek opinions. We should be glad that he did not. The insincerity of such opinions would probably have been all too apparent, and the spirit of the play—which perhaps, in the last analysis, depends on sincerity—would have lost more than it would have gained by the concession. There are limits beyond which a true artist cannot follow 'best example.'

That Milton felt himself justified in expressing un-Hellenic views in a classical form is quite apparent. *Paradise Lost* is a magnificent case in point. In the preface to *Samson Agonistes* he offers an indirect explanation:

> The Apostle *Paul* himself thought it not unworthy to insert a verse of *Euripides* into the Text of Holy Scripture, I *Cor.* 15. 33. and *Paræus* commenting on the *Revelation,* divides the whole Book as a Tragedy, into Acts distinguisht each by a Chorus of Heavenly Harpings and Song between. . . . *Gregory Nazianzen* a Father of the Church, thought it not unbeseeming the sanctity of his person to write a Tragedy, which he entitl'd, *Christ suffering.*

In *The Reason of Church Government* Milton is more definite:

> That what the greatest and choycest wits of *Athens* . . . did for their country, I in my proportion with this over and above of being a Christian, might doe for mine.[29]

Later he specifically mentions 'those Dramatick constitutions, wherein *Sophocles* and *Euripides* raigne.' And the conclusion of this passage is significant:

> These abilities, wheresover they be found, are the inspired guift of God . . . and are of power beside the office of a pulpit, to inbreed and cherish in a great people the seeds of vertu, and publick civility, to allay the perturbations of the mind, and set the affections in right tune, to celebrate in glorious and lofty Hymns the throne and equipage of Gods Almightinesse, and what he works, and what he suffers to be wrought with high providence. . . .[30]

Let us notice that in this place Milton asserts the power of tragedy (and, indeed, of all poetry) 'to allay the perturbations of the mind.' This brings us to the last of our five aspects of tone. Attic drama is sublime. It manages, somehow, to lift us above the agonies it depicts.

[29] 1641 ed., p. 38; Bohn ii, 478.
[30] 1641 ed., p. 39; Bohn ii, 479.

It is more than stirring; it is spiritually elevating. Many reasons may be assigned for this, and any of them—or all of them—may be correct. Perhaps it is because we witness, to borrow Jebb's phrase, 'an ideal grandeur of agony.' Perhaps it is because everything vulgar and mean has been excluded. Perhaps the ancient poets were deliberately bringing about a katharsis. And, even more likely, perhaps we are carried beyond pain and despair on the wings of magnificent poetry. When all is said, we may be indebted to consummate art for our release. Certainly, in the kind of tragedy we are considering, we not only are brought face to face with the problem of human misery; there is always 'something that makes it endurable.' It may be, as Lucas suggests, merely 'the thought that the hero, like Samson, has at least got cleanly off the stage.' [31] But whatever its cause, Milton has caught this spirit in *Samson Agonistes*. It is a fact which does not lend itself easily to proof, for the individual's impression must be the ultimate test. But nothing I have thus far encountered in criticism has led me to doubt the validity of my own experience.

Finally, let me make very clear a point which, in order to simplify my discussion, I have so far ignored. The Greek spirit—other than aesthetic—is a combination, a blend, of all the aspects we have been considering, and doubtless of many more. It is possible to find un-Hellenic drama which possesses one or more of these qualities; it is the combination which is truly Hellenic. Shakespearian tragedy is both thoughtful and sublime; but it is not didactic or religious or serious in the Greek way. Certain religious dramas, such as those of Calderon, are deficient in depth and meaning. In more modern tragedies, the note of sublimity is tragically absent. At best we can say, with regard to artists like Ibsen and Tchekov, that we are inspired by 'the sheer integrity which faces life as it is.' [32] But much has disappeared—and it is not merely splendor. Milton was one of the last men whose intellect comprehended all the aspects of the Greek spirit and whose genius caught that spirit in a piece of living art.

[31] F. L. Lucas, *Tragedy in Relation to Aristotle's 'Poetics'* (London: L. and V. Woolf, 1928), p. 59.

[32] Lucas, *Tragedy*, p. 59.

# The Epithet *Agonistes*

## by F. Michael Krouse

Critics have paid little attention to the epithet *Agonistes* which Milton applied to Samson in the title of the tragedy. Bishop Newton thought that the term was used to designate Samson as an actor, or as one represented in a play. Dunster eschewed Newton's interpretation and declared that *Agonistes* refers to Samson's being brought forth "to exhibit his athletick powers." Dunster also remarked that the epithet served to define the scope of the play, just as Aeschylus distinguished *Prometheus Bound* from *Prometheus Unbound*.[1] Masson accepted Dunster's interpretation and simply noted in passing that *Agonistes* means "the Agonist, Athlete or Wrestler." [2] Verity repeated this gloss, adding that *Agonistes* means "a combatant at public games" and that it emphasizes "the main aspect under which Samson appears," namely, "as wrestler before the assembled Philistines." [3] Professor [Merritt] Hughes perpetuated this venerable interpretation in his recent edition of the tragedy. "*Agonistes,*" he says, "transliterates the Greek name for the amateur athletes who competed in the public games, and it refers to Samson's appearance at the festival of the Philistines in the temple of Dagon at the climax of the tragedy, when he wrestles with the pillars there." [4] Professor [William R.] Parker, however, has declared that Samson Agonistes is "more than Samson the Wrestler," reminding us that *Agonistes* means also "an advocate, an actor, and a champion." He even suggests that when Milton used the

"*The Epithet* Agonistes." *From Chap. IV, "Milton's Samson and the Tradition" in* F. M. Krouse, Milton's Samson and the Christian Tradition. (*Princeton: Princeton University Press for the University of Cincinnati, 1949*). Copyright © *1949 by the* Princeton University Press. Reprinted by permission of the publisher.

[1] Todd, ed., *Works of Milton* (London: 1809), V, 343.

[2] *Works of Milton* (London: The Macmillan Co., 1890), II, 582.

[3] *Milton's "Samson Agonistes"* (Cambridge: Cambridge University Press, 1932), p. 60.

[4] *Paradise Regained, the Mirror Poems and Samson Agonistes,* ed. Merritt Y. Hughes (New York: Odyssey Press, 1937), p. 537, n. 1.

epithet he may have had in mind the English words *agony* and *agonize*. But he concludes his consideration of the title by confessing that he regards such attempts to interpret *Agonistes* as "futile guesses." [5]

There is, however, ample evidence in both Graeco-Roman and Christian traditions to enable us to find a more accurate and meaningful interpretation of the title of Milton's tragedy than these, and without resort to guesswork. In fact, when one approaches it with the Christian tradition in mind, the title is like a wide gate opening upon the total meaning of the poem. I shall try here to show that when Milton used the epithet *Agonistes* he probably intended it both to denote a specific conception of Samson and to connote a view of life which was then twenty-three centuries old. In order to regain the now-forgotten connotations of *Agonistes,* it is necessary to examine the history of a group of Greek and Latin words and to consider their significance in Christian literature and Christian doctrine during the Middle Ages and the Reformation.

*Agonistes* is, as Professor Hughes has said, a transliteration of the Greek word ἀγωνιστής [agonistes], which was in turn derived from the word ἀγών [agon]. The earliest meanings of ἀγών [agon] were purely literal: it denoted (1) a gathering or assembly to see games, (2) the arena itself where the games were held, or (3) the contest for a prize at public games. However, like many such words, ἀγών [agon] and its synonyms and derivatives soon acquired, by extension, metaphorical meanings which ultimately supplanted the literal; hence ἀγών [agon] was widely used to denote (4) any struggle or trial, but increasingly (5) a spiritual struggle, an inner conflict. The word ἆθλον [athlon], too, which in its older form (ἄεθλον) [aethlon] had meant simply a physical combat, came to be used only in the sense of "spiritual struggle." [6]

The grounds of this semantic amelioration can be found in Greek philosophic writings. Among the fragments of the pre-Socratics, for example, there is an elegy by Xenophanes, the poet-philosopher of the sixth century, in which is stated for the first time the ideal of philosophic wisdom in explicit opposition to the ideal of mere physical prowess. Looking upon athletes performing in the games, Xenophanes was filled with contempt, and in this elegy he expressed his conviction that mere quickness of foot would never suffice to establish order and

[5] William R. Parker, *Milton's Debt to Greek Tragedy* (Baltimore: Johns Hopkins Press, 1937), p. 13.

[6] See H. G. Liddell and Robert Scott, *Greek-English Lexicon,* ed. Sir H. S. Jones (Oxford, 1940).

justice in the state. Using the terminology of the public games metaphorically, he pleaded for the inception of a new ideal which would exalt and reward athletes of the mind and spirit rather than athletes of the body. These philosopher-athletes, he argued—not the runners, the wrestlers, and the horsemen—should be granted the most generous prizes the state can provide.[7] Many Hellenists today believe that it was during the century after Xenophanes that this ideal came as near establishment as it was ever to come in the history of man. It is certain that during the great period of Greece no less a figure than the Platonic Socrates devoted his life to the doctrine that only lovers of ideas can be wise, that only the pursuit of wisdom makes human life meaningful or death understandable. Nor did Socrates think of philosophy in passive terms. In his valediction in the *Phaedo* (90e), as in many other utterances, he expressed the business of the philosopher in terms of contest, struggle, or strife, urging his disciples to play the man and seek strenuously for soundness of mind (ἀνδριστέον καὶ προθυμητέον ὑγιῶς ἔχειν). The Platonic ethic favored the contemplative life, but it was to be lived in a state of intellectual and spiritual *agon:* only by extraordinary and long-continued exertion of mind and spirit could the lover of ideas hope to break through the phenomenal world to know the Good and the True. In the *Laws* (731a) the Athenian Stranger counselled his hearers to strive with all their might for virtue and wisdom, and Socrates himself concluded that unforgettable conversation recorded in the *Republic* by exhorting his followers to

> hold fast ever to the heavenly way and follow after justice and virtue always, considering that the soul is immortal and able to endure every sort of good and every sort of evil. Thus shall we live dear to one another and to the gods, both while remaining here and when, like conquerors in the games [τὰ ἆθλα . . . οἱ νικηφόροι] who go round to gather gifts, we receive our reward.[8]

[7]      ῥώμης γὰρ ἀμείνων
ἀνδρῶν ἠδ᾽ ἵππων ἡμετέρη σοφίη.
ἀλλ᾽ εἰκῆ μάλα τοῦτο νομίζεται, οὐδὲ δίκαιον
προκρίνειν ῥώμην τῆς ἀγαθῆς σοφίης.
["... for the poet's skill is better than the strength of men and horses. 'Tis very unconsidered, the custom of man in this matter; it is not right that strength should be judged worthier than (noble) skill." *Elegy and Iambus*, I, ed. J. M. Edmonds, Loeb Classical Library, 1901, pp. 194-5—ED.] In *Die Fragmente der Vorsokratiker,* ed. Hermann Diels and Walther Kranz, 5th ed. (Berlin, 1934), I, 129.

[8] *Republic* (621d), trans. Jowett.

Such widely known passages in Hellenic philosophy reveal a concept of life as *agon* which suffered sea-changes and outlived its proponents by many centuries. . . .

So it was, too, for St. Paul, Tertullian, Cyprian, Lactantius, Prudentius, Augustine, Isidore of Seville, and numerous other Christian writers.[9] St. Paul's concept of "the good fight of faith" is but the earliest and best known manifestation of the Christian adoption of this ideal which had originated among the virtuous pagans. Indeed, the *agon*-idea took its place very close to the heart of Christianity, especially during the period in which the Christian Church was consciously making its way to a spiritual hegemony *contra haereticos* of whatever coloring. But there is an even more significant respect in which the *agon*-concept was close to the heart of Christianity.

In an admirable historical study of the Christian doctrine of Atonement, Gustaf Aulén, the Swedish theologian, has pointed out that of all the interpretations of Christ's propitiation of God for the Redemption of Man, only one is ancient enough and persistent enough to be termed "the classical idea of the Atonement." This was not the "subjective" theory, which dates only from the age of the Schoolmen; neither was it the "exemplarist" theory, which developed among the "liberal" theologians of the Enlightenment. The theory which Aulén calls "classical" was first fully formed by Irenaeus, prevailed during the first ten centuries of the Christian era, was revived by Luther, and remained a central tenet of "orthodox" Protestant theology in the sixteenth and seventeenth centuries. According to this "classical" theory, Christ propitiated God and redeemed Man by struggling against evil, by waging war against the powers of darkness to which Man had

---

[9] Cf. the long article on *agon* in the sense of "pugnis spiritalibus, de persecutionibus et martyrio" [the spiritual struggles deriving from persecutions and martyrdom] in *Thesaurus Linguae Latinae* (Leipzig, 1900), I, 1411 f. There are many more references to the *agon*-idea in medieval Christian literature than can be taken into account here. All Christian usage of the words ἀγών, *agon*, ἀγωνιστής, *agonista*, ἀθλητής, *athleta* which I have explored points to the conclusions presented here, where only a sampling of that literature is possible. Cf. Stauffer's article on ἀγών in *Theologisches Wörterbuch zum Neuen Testament*, ed. G. Kittel (Stuttgart, 1933), I, 134-40. Professor T. S. K. Scott-Craig called my attention to this article of Stauffer's.

One curious use of the word *agon* may be found in Ambrose (*Epist. XIX, 22*), who gives the translation "Agon" for the word *Lehi* in Judges 15:14 and adds that it is so called "to this day" because "ibi Samson gloriosum certamen virtute egregia consummaverit" [. . . there Samson completed the glorious struggle with extraordinary moral virtue—ED.] (*Certamen* is, of course, a common synonym for *agon*.)

been enslaved ever since the Fall. Aulén shows that out of writings in which Christ's mission was expressed in military, athletic, forensic, or dramatic terms arose a conception of *Christus Victor,* who came off triumphantly from his encounter with Satan in the wilderness.[10] My own investigations support Aulén's conclusions. Throughout medieval ecclesiastical literature, the *agon*-idea is found to be completely assimilated by Christianity. Christ is often given the epithet *athleta,* and all the saints come to be written of in similar terms. Among the medieval writers who gave this cast to Christ's victory over Satan were Jerome, Bede, Strabo, Rupert of St. Heribert, and Chrysostom. And in the sixteenth and seventeenth centuries John Knox, Lancelot Andrewes, John Fisher, Franciscus Luca, John Downame, and Thomas Fuller wrote of Christ's encounter with Satan in terms of conflict.[11] This imagery was extended early to all the saints. . . .* In fact, these words are used so interchangeably that it is not possible to regard the conceptions of *miles Christianus, athleta Christianus,* and *agonista Christianus* as in any real sense separate or distinct.

[10] *Christus Victor: an Historical Study of the Three Main Types of the Idea of the Atonement,* trans. A. G. Hebert (London, 1931), *passim.* An even more exhaustive study of the history of the theory of Christ's Atonement is Elizabeth Marie Pope's *"Paradise Regained": the Tradition and the Poem* (Baltimore, 1947). Professor Pope devotes a section of her final chapter to an examination of the combat images used "whenever the theologians of the Middle Ages or the Renaissance turn to imagery to describe the temptation." As she shows, these writers almost invariably "think and write of it as if it were a struggle between rival warriors or athletes."

[11] Jerome, *Commentarii in Evangelium Matthaei (Pat. Lat.,* XXVI, 31); Bede, *In Matthaei Evangelium Expositio (Pat. Lat.,* XCII, 18); Strabo, *Expositio in Quatuor Evangelia (Pat. Lat.,* CXIV, 870); Rupert of St. Heribert, *In Quatuor Evangelistarum Commentariorum Liber (Pat. Lat.,* CLXVII, 1547); Chrysostom, *Homiliae in Matthaeum (Pat. Graec.,* LVII, 210); John Knox, *A Notable and Comfortable Exposition of M. John Knoxes, upon the Fourth of Matthew, concerning the Tentation* [sic.] *of Christ* (London, 1583), in *Works,* ed. David Laing (Edinburgh, 1856), IV, 103; Lancelot Andrewes, *Seven Sermons on the Wonderful Combat, for God's Glory and Man's Salvation, between Christ and Satan* (first ed. 1592), in *Ninety-six Sermons,* ed. John Parkinson (Oxford, 1841-1843), p. 480; John Fisher, *Analysis Logica Libri S. Lucae* (London, 1597), p. 57; Franciscus Luca, *In Lucam Commentaria* (first ed. 1606), in *Scripturae Sacrae Cursus Completus,* ed. J. P. Migne (Paris, 1862), XXII, 527; John Downame, *The Christian Warfare* (London, 1612), p. 15; and Thomas Fuller, *A Comment on the Eleven First Verses of the Fourth Chapter of S. Matthew's Gospel, concerning Christ's Temptations, delivered in XII Sermons* (London, 1652), pp. 1 ff.

* A brief catalogue showing the extension of this imagery to saints has been omitted—ED.

# The Idea as Pattern:
# Despair and *Samson Agonistes*

## *by Don Cameron Allen*

Despair is as proper to Hell as black fire, but living men can cir-
cumvent this evil. Even Judas and Cain, whom Milton mentions in his
account of despair,[1] were not in their life-times beyond the limits of
grace, and it is with the living, not with those desperadoes of eternity,
that Milton is concerned. It is they whom Milton would rescue, for, as
the theologians inform us, there is no salvation for them who die in
despair. Hence, if the reader is to be here taught a Christian lesson,
Milton must translate the matter into human symbols. . . .

I expect that Milton saw in the fable that he invented for the tenth
book [of *Paradise Lost*] a kind of moral narrative. Despair, sprouting
from sin and from a sense of unworthiness or from an unknowingness
of mercy, is for corporeal man supreme disobedience to the will of
God. If he continues in this state of spiritual sloth, the mind of man
will turn to the death-hunger which may propel him, as Saul was
propelled, into damnation as complete and eternal as that of the
demons. The soul cure is simple. Patiently and obediently man must
await the revelation of God's will supported by an extraordinary
confidence in divine love and mercy. Adam comes eventually to this
conclusion and he is rewarded with a prophetic vision that makes
patience easier and obedience more sure. But Milton is never content
to make a point once or to make it in a subordinate fashion; he
elaborates this theme in *Samson Agonistes,* which is his proudest analy-

---

[1] *De doctrina Christiana, Works* (New York: Columbia University Press, 1931),
XVII, 56-8.

sis of the problem of Christian despair. I shall begin my explication by discarding.

First, I am sure that Milton's self-identification with the young judge of Israel did much to raise the character of that primitive ruffian of a half-savage legend to nobler heights than the compilers of the Book of Judges could possibly imagine. The hairy sun symbol of the oldest of Jewish myths, who seems so repulsive to those who do not read his story with sanctified inattention, becomes in the great tragic poem a mighty Christian hero, worthy of all those prophetic embellishments with which a thousand years of Christian exegesis had adorned him. Yet the whole intent of the tragedy has been somewhat obscured by some scholars who are more interested in autobiography than in poetry. Certainly Milton was blind, certainly he thought of himself as God's champion among a faithless people, but to say this is merely to conclude that he found the legend of Samson a congenial subject. This is possibly the first rule of artistic effort, but not its end.

In general the slight critical literature on this poem centers about the alterations in the protagonist's character as a species of continual rebuke to Johnson's complaint that "the intermediate parts have neither cause nor consequence, neither hasten nor retard the catastrophe." I should like to join this movement, but I cannot promise to keep step. By carefully describing Samson's slow-witted realization of the fact that he is God's man against the Philistine's Dagon, critics have revealed a dramatic pattern that Johnson overlooked. This pattern certainly exists, but it is not the only center about which the verse of the tragedy turns. The remarks of the other characters and of the choruses have long been thought of as goads to Samson's progress and as hindrances, too, but I am not completely convinced of this. Krouse has recently analyzed these tragic conditions in terms of an accepted theory of temptation which is illustrated in both *Paradise Lost* and *Paradise Regained*. For him Samson becomes intermediate in the chronology of Satanic enticements, and we as Christian readers are given a third and perhaps ultimate example of how we also may withstand the blandishments of evil.[2] The tragedy can be thought of in this way; in fact, it may be part of a tetralogy that includes *Comus*, but the temptations are somewhat different. So without rejecting any

[2] *Milton's Samson and the Christian Tradition* (Princeton: Princeton University Press for University of Cincinnati, 1949), pp. 124-32; see also Elizabeth Pope, *Paradise Regained: The Tradition and the Poem* (Baltimore: Johns Hopkins Press, 1947), pp. 51-107.

other explanations, I should like to shift the emphases a little because the artistic process that I notice in *Samson* centers on the regeneration of a desperate man and includes in its circular scope all of the theological dicta on the genesis and cure of despair.

When we study the documents in the Samson tradition, we are disturbed by one question that was constantly phrased and that makes the theological dissertations on this legend particularly unique. "Was Samson," the theologians ask, "a suicide and does his soul wander beyond the pales of mercy?" Though sometimes implicit, this question rests on Samson's last words which are recorded in the authoritative Hebrew text and expunged with vainly suppressed horror in the vernacular translations: "Let my soul," Samson prays as he braces himself between the pillars, "die with the Philistines." Either Samson did not believe in the after-life or he was praying, as a self-convicted suicide, for release from the pains of Hell. We can imagine the confusion of Christian men who could read the Hebrew; the passage must either be emended as a scribal error or sacredly misread. The controversy about Samson's suicide may be followed through the history of Christian hermeneutics, but there is no need to trace every step of the way in this essay since two contemporaries of Milton summarize the opposing cases. John Donne, by confuting the arguments of the orthodox, upholds Samson as the first of Biblical suicides and a justifier of self-destruction.[3] Franciscus Collius[4] gathers together the contrary testimony to show that Samson died a martyred avenger of Israel's Jehovah. Milton, we can be sure, knew this contention well, for he recognizes it poetically in the warning words that he places in the mouth of the aged and half-comprehending Manoa.

> Be penitent and for thy faults contrite,
> But act not in thy own affliction, Son;
> Repent the sin, but if the punishment
> Thou canst avoid, self-preservation bids;
> Or th' execution leave to high disposal,
> And let another hand, not thine, exact
> Thy penal forfeit from thyself (502-508).

But Manoa is wrong, for Milton's Samson, as Milton's Adam, is desperate and the desire to die is his, but death by suicide is never in his mind.

The eating despair of Samson is partially unveiled in his first speech

[3] *Biathanatos* (London, 1648), pp. 199-201.
[4] *De Animabus Paganorum* (Mediolani, 1622), pp. 251-9.

where, unlike his prototype, he shows himself to be a man of "restless thoughts" that fill his mind with doubts. For what purpose, he asks himself, was I singled out, "separate to God," I who am "eyeless in Gaza at the mill with slaves?" This, to a reader of seventeenth-century essays on Providence, is a familiar line of reasoning; it is the way the good man talks in his tribulations. Job asked questions of this sort, and Milton knew that it was the first move in the gambit of doubts about the wisdom and validity of Providence. For a moment Samson is on the edge of error, but he saves himself with a quick admonition. "But peace, I must not quarrel with the will/Of highest dispensation" (60-61).

Yet there is a fluctuation throughout the early part of the tragedy in Samson's attitude towards himself, a fluctuation arising from the contention between his sense of sin and the fear that he has been abandoned by God. The seventeenth century knew that the most righteous men were sometimes keenly aware of a separation from God, that even God himself could cry at the ninth hour, "Eli, eli, lama, sabachthani." But there is a difference between this feeling of desertion and the one that arises from a guilty heart; hence, Samson, as blind in eye as he was once in mind, has this more quickened conviction of abandonment.

With this the death-thought comes, for the darkness of his physical affliction symbolizes for Samson the darkness of the pit of death (100-104). His face becomes the mirror of his mind as the chorus sorrowfully describes him "As one past hope, abandon'd, and by himself given o'er." For these Hebrews of the year 1199 B.C. (I follow the chronology of Salianus) Samson appears, as mediaeval men were to see him, a broken giant from some titanic *de casibus virorum* (166-75). "Deject not then so overmuch thyself" (213). Samson hardly needs this advice; he blames himself for giving up his "fort of silence to a Woman," but he blames Israel more for hanging back when deliverance was at hand at Lehi. At this moment the inward undulation of Samson's spirit is upward, and this is good because Manoa's visit will once again bring him to the edge of the chasm of despair.

Manoa has much of the pessimism and some of the world pain of a man who has lived long and seen most of his hopes thin out; hence, he has become, as much as it is possible for a Jew, a pre-Stoa stoic who sees in withdrawal, in the quiet folding of hands, the decent and sensible conduct of life. From time to time his suffering finds voice: "And oh, what not in man/Deceivable and vain!" (349-50). But love is strong in him for his strong son; it is, in fact, so strong that sometimes he doubts the justice of God (368-72). Wanting in a correct conception of God's wondrous ways, Manoa unwittingly substitutes himself for God, and seeks to persuade his son to accept the plans of a loving father instead of awaiting those of a loving God. If there is a temptation in this scene, it revolves about this substitute proposal. Had Samson, who has already fallen into sloth through lechery (Aquinas states that *"delectationes venereae"* pave the way to sloth), accepted his father's plans, he would have plunged deeper in the slough of sloth. Yet Manoa, in his old man's fashion, goes beyond this. By implying that God has no further use for Samson, he presses his son against the sharp blade of despair. God, says Manoa, who is truly more blind than Samson, will surely assert his might against Dagon;

> But for thee what shall be done?
> Thou must not in the meanwhile here forgot
> Lie in this miserable loathsome plight
> Neglected (478-81).

The ultimate victory of Jehovah is never doubted by either Samson or his father, but they are both totally unaware of the instrument of God's impending success. As a consequence of this ignorance, Manoa's love and devotion—emotions good in themselves—have the attributes of temptation, for the eventuation of these humanly good impulses is the thwarting of the divinely good.

During the whole of this first scene, Samson's self-accusations pile up. "Now I have sinned; now I am damned." Not the least among the items of his personal indictment is the feeling that his sick doubts have infected the nation whose champion he was.

> To *Israel*, diffidence of God, and doubt
> In feeble hearts, propense enough before
> To waver, or fall off and join with Idols (454-56).

Joined with this widening feeling of guilt is the lingering notion, for which Manoa is partly responsible, that God intends to punish him but not to employ him (487-501). When Samson puts this hard intimation into words, his father instinctively frames another temptation. By warning Samson against suicide, he puts the thought in his mind. But though Samson, at those words, begins to be hungry for "oft-invocated death" and says of life "To what end should I seek it?" (522), he prefers that death will find him worn out at the mill rather than sitting in "sedentary numbness" at home. Neither suicide nor sloth are in his mind.

Manoa is probably Milton's broadest irony. His well meant attempts to alleviate the suffering of his son have invariably an effect of contrary intent. The loving vision of a helpless and hopeless idleness extending into a long old age that is his only medicine for the convalescent Samson almost produced a dangerous relapse.

> So much I feel genial spirits droop,
> My hopes all flat, nature within me seems
> In all her functions weary of herself;
> My race of glory run, and race of shame,
> And I shall shortly be with them that rest (594-98).

Once again Samson is beset by a "sense of Heav'n's desertion" (632) and despair, black and ugly, fells him as no strong man had ever done.

> Nor am I in the list of them that hope;
> Hopeless are all my evils, all remediless;
> This one prayer yet remains, might I be heard,
> No long petition, speedy death,
> The close of all my miseries, and the balm (647-51).

So Samson reaches the bottom level of despair; he will never again sink so low. The sickness is so regnant in him that its contagion begets a similar disease in the chorus, the symptoms of which are its complaint against the Jehovah who persecutes his elect and its prayer that Samson may be spared. The complaint is artistically ironic because it exactly marks the point in the tragedy where the regeneration of the protagonist begins. The former emotional fluctuations of the hero will cease with the last note of the choral song and Samson will move steadily upward towards the elected event that will make him God's martyred champion and one of the great prototypes of Christ. The irony is not diminished with this scene for it permeates the whole regenerative process, which depends not on the counsel of Manoa or the Hebraic chorus, Samson's friends and the children of Jehovah, but rather on the taunts of Dalila and Harapha, enemies of Israel and haters of Jehovah. For Milton, God had, indeed, a bitter sense of humor.

By refusing the lazy comforts offered by his father, Samson implicitly demonstrates that the love of God is to be preferred to paternal affection. The first enticement to sloth is forfended and with it the avenue to the damnable sin of despair is stopped. The same pattern of distraction from the foreordained triumph is poetically repeated in the scene with Dalila, save that in this episode the temptation is one of venereal love, that fostress of despair. This is an old weakness of Samson's; he had been tangled in it before.

But we cannot understand this episode in its full import unless we accept all that Dalila says as seriously spoken. Her final speech has always been allowed to color everything that she says, and this, I think, is not only a critical error in the commentaries, but a failure to read dramatically. When Dalila leaves the stage, she is a spurned beauty, a wife rejected. Her consolation, as she proclaims it, is the prospect of political renown. I see no reason, then, to assume that all of her speeches except the last are lies and that the whole purpose of her visit is to twit Samson. This would suggest that Dalila has a higher type of intelligence than that with which Milton ordinarily endows her sex. Shallow though she is, Dalila visits Samson out of contrition and remorse, her kind of contrition and remorse, but Samson himself knows that these emotions are but thinly part of her and that the real impulsion is lechery.

> But Love constrain'd thee; call it furious rage
> To satisfy thy lust (836-37).

By rejecting her, Samson expiates, among other evils, his own history of lechery.

Every speech of Dalila's except the last is filled with verbal tones of contrition; and if we consider all of this spurious, we lose the intensity of the total contention. We must assume that while this charmer of charmers is speaking, Samson is aware of a strong physical attraction made more persuasive by redolent memories. The old passion is perhaps even more intense because now, for the first time, Dalila's natural gift for feminine cajolery and sweet words is enhanced by a feeling of guilt for her treachery and of sympathy for the betrayed. Granted that these emotions are all on the surface; nonetheless, they are as deeply felt as Dalila can feel. If we will be just a little tender with this "Hyaena," we can readily understand the pressures under which the fragile resistance of her slender intelligence collapsed. She wanted to know her husband's secret; she knew him to be a fickle lover; she feared for the seemingly reckless man who fought lions and armies single-handed; she was overwhelmed by the prestige of princes and archbishops, by Church and State. Eve betrayed her husband on the fair say-so of a beast of the fields and Eve was the nearest thing to feminine perfection that God ever created. Let us give Dalila a little chivalrous indulgence.

As *advocatus Dalilae* I may say still more. When Samson makes surly mock of her remorse and sarcastically shreds with his wise piety her self-exculpating brief, she patiently persists in her solicitations.

> Life yet hath many solaces, enjoy'd
> Where other senses want not their delights
> At home in leisure and domestic ease,
> Exempt from many a care and chance to which
> Eye-sight exposes daily men abroad.
> I to the Lords will intercede, not doubting
> Their favourable ear, that I may fetch thee
> From forth this loathsome prison-house to abide
> With me, where my redoubl'd love and care
> With nursing diligence, to me glad office,
> May ever tend about thee to old age
> With all things grateful cheer'd, and so supplied,
> That what by me thou hast lost thou least shall miss
>
> (915-27).

One can reasonably doubt whether a woman who came, as the critics say, to gloat over the misery of the husband whom she hated, a woman who did not believe in her own sincerity, would make such a selfless proposal to a broken and blinded man. We should also remember that her anger does not flare when Samson scornfully and even nastily rejects her offer. It is only when he spurns her last and, to her, most powerful enticement, physical contact ("Let me approach at least, and touch thy hand"), that she loses her rather remarkable self-control. To her complete confusion, she learns that she is physically repellent to Samson. For a wife or mistress this must be the ultimate insult. If we are to question any one of Dalila's announcements, it is the last one that she utters when she leaves the scene escorted by her wounded pride. The reward of a footnote in the history of the Phoenicians, which she says will now be hers, is sorry consolation, indeed, for the sort of woman who had been an international beauty.

The importance of this scene is manifest. Samson asserts himself against his first antagonist, and by this simple but energetic action the dejection, in which his interview with the comforting Manoa left him, vanishes. His uxorious weakness, the mother of much of his despair, goes with Dalila's exit. He has found the woman out, so he talks like a monastic brother. She is a Circe, who with her "enchanting cup, and warbling charms," has transformed him into a manless thing. She is a viper, too, a reptile that destroys her mate in the act of love. Samson discovers all of this as he struggles to free himself from the trap of Dalila's body. The chorus is not insensitive to the struggle.

> Yet beauty, though injurious, hath strange power,
> After offence returning, to regain
> Love once possest, nor can be easily
> Repuls't, without much inward passion felt
> And secret sting of amorous remorse (1003-1007).

Samson feels these emotions, but he has withstood the solicitations of paternal affection and has less difficulty in rejecting those of venereal love. He is walking towards purification and the right understanding of the love of God, and in this scene, he wins a test victory, the first of a series, against Dagon and his vain adorers. I do not think that temptation is the basic motif of this episode; it is intended as an adumbration of Samson's ultimate triumph. Dalila is withstood, but we must remember that both she and Harapha will finally be overwhelmed in the fall of Dagon's house.

During the subsequent scene with the giant Harapha, Samson arises still higher in godly confidence and almost leaves his original despondency behind. His contention with Dalila enables him to suppress his erstwhile lechery; the conflict with Harapha will enable him to subdue his apathy. Boughner sees in this event a comic moment, a period of relief before the final tragedy, and compares Harapha to the famous *milites gloriosi* of literature.[5] In these comparisons he seeks a means of enriching [William R.] Parker's prior theory that Harapha was a blusterer similar to those found in Greek and Latin tragedy.[6] I doubt that Milton, who had complained in his preface about those who "through the poet's error" intermixed "comic stuff with tragic sadness and gravity," would make the same error himself. I likewise doubt that Harapha is similar to Ralph Roister Doister, his ancestors or his progeny. We should accept Milton's prefatory remarks as sincere—[Daniel C.] Boughner does not—and, as a consequence, we shall want Harapha to be as sincere as his inventor.

If we will read without prejudgment, we will discover that Harapha's

---

[5] "Milton's Harapha and Renaissance Comedy," *English Literary History*, XI (1944), pp. 297-306.
[6] *Milton's Debt to Greek Tragedy in Samson Agonistes* (Baltimore: Johns Hopkins Press, 1937), p. 122.

first speech is that of a genuinely valorous man, proud of his famous
ancestry and of his long record in the annals of war. We know his
counterparts in the romances of chivalry—knights who know their
rivals by reputation but who have never competed with them in the
lists or on the fields of honor. Harapha's visit to Samson is prompted
by a champion's curiosity, and we should accept his first speeches as
uttered honestly and generously. When he says he regrets that he cannot win honor from Samson in "mortal duel" because Samson is blind,
he is not hedging but talking as a man conscious of the knightly code.
If we insist that Harapha is a coward or a blusterer from the moment
of his entrance, we fail to understand the essential purpose of the whole
tragic situation. If, on the other hand, we admit his sincerity, the scene
becomes infinitely important because we can watch the degeneration of
Harapha's courage. Before our eyes a brave and knightly man will
change into a coward and a blusterer. This amazing alteration in character, brought about by Samson's growing confidence in Jehovah and
Harapha's intimation of the supernatural power apparent in Samson,
tells us more than even the verse implies of God's impending triumph.

As Samson hurls challenge after challenge at Harapha, "his Giant-
ship's" valour withers and he begins to think of all the excuses and
dodges that had been used by generations of craven warriors to save
themselves from an unlucky contest. The alteration in Harapha's nature is really a miracle which establishes its validity by taking place
in our presence. The grand champion of Gath (and he did not get this
title by bragging) turns into a snivelling bully-boy; Lancelot becomes
Braggadocchio within the space of a hundred and fifty lines. Samson's
confidence grows and Harapha's melts. To defend his own declining
courage, Harapha uses some of the old arguments that had earlier cast
Samson into despair. God has disowned you, says he,

> Thee he regards not, owns not, hath cut off
> Quite from his people, and delivered up
> Into thy Enemies' hand, . . .
> As good for nothing else (1157-59, 63).

But Samson knows better now; the theme of divine abandonment has
no effect. God, Samson intones, has afflicted me justly, but he has not
deserted me:

> yet despair not of his final pardon
> Whose ear is ever open; and his eye
> Gracious to re-admit the suppliant;

> In confidence whereof I once again
> Defy thee to the trial of mortal fight,
> By combat to decide whose god is God,
> Thine or whom I with *Israel's* Sons adore (1171-77).

With this speech we know that Samson will not die an apathetic death. Life has returned to him; and though he does not yet know how it will all be brought about, he is God's champion once more. There is no temptation in this scene and no comedy; it is the most important scene of all, for it is the hinge of the tragedy. By the victory over Harapha, who symbolizes all that is valiant in Philistia, God, working through Samson, has put Dagon down. It is, in truth, the final event of the tragedy in miniature.

Now Samson's course is easy, for the way upward, the patient surrender to faith, once the obstacles in the hard lower levels are cleared, is as easy as the effortless descent to despair. Harapha is the dramatic link between the last breath of desperation,

> But come what will, my deadliest foe will prove
> My speediest friend, by death to rid me hence,
> The worst that he can give, to me the best (1262-64);

and the triumphant death, of which he is, perhaps, the bringer-on. "He will directly to the Lords, I fear,/And with malicious counsels stir them up/Some way or other yet further to afflict thee" (1250-52). Samson will still hesitate because he is a strict keeper of the Law, but his reasons for hesitation will vanish as soon as he, like the Christ of *Paradise Regained*, trusts again his inward impulses. "I begin to feel/Some rousing motions in me which dispose/To something extraordinary my thoughts" (1381-83). We know the nature of this "motion."

> And now by some strong motion I am led
> Into this Wilderness, to what intent
> I learn not yet; perhaps I need not know;
> For what concerns my knowledge God reveals
>                              (*PR*, I. 290-93).

With these words God's athlete enters the ranks of the blessed.

Samson's God-given victory over Dagon and the flower of Philistia is, according to Milton's dramatic intent, not so great as Samson's conquest of doubt and despair. The final act stemming from this conquest destroys the universal doubt about the wisdom of God's Providence which had invaded Israel, the doubt for which Samson blamed himself in his earlier moments of dejection. The chorus exults in the clearing of this doubt and the final unfolding of God's plan, and in so doing exonerates the wrestler of God from the taint of suicide. "Among thy slain self-kill'd/Not willingly, but tangl'd in the fold/Of dire necessity" (1664-66). Manoa, too, is purged of his dubious fears.

> And which is best and happiest yet, all this
> With God not parted from him, as was fear'd,
> But favouring and assisting to the end (1718-20).

But there is more to the tragedy than the passionate purgation of the chorus, of Manoa, and of Samson. Aristotle may have laid down the rules and the poet Milton may have obeyed them, but behind them both was a greater critic and a greater poet who made the rules in eternity and supplied the tragic *fabula* for his own glory. Now that the happy catastrophe has occurred and the final chorus is sung, the candles are burning out in the long hall and the spectators are departing surer of the wisdom of the great artist whom Milton served.

> His servants he with new acquist
> Of true experience from this great event
> With peace and consolation hath dismist,
> And calm of mind, all passion spent.

# The Return of Samson

## by *Arnold Stein*

The tide has turned. Now there is no doubt. A few last counter-motions persist, but they exert no convincing pull. They ripple the surface here and there, and make a few slapping sounds to mark their own indecision before they succumb utterly to the irresistible force growing beneath them. But we are strangers, as always, to the inlet of individual human experience. We have come, and in a condensed period of time have been able to mark many of the formations revealed and partly revealed by the ebb, along with certain historical signs remaining from the flood. But the speed of the flux and the immediate details of its course we cannot know. And as the event we have waited for is finally about to happen, we are moved back from it, so that when we return it will be to experience the most revealing moment of time. (And facing the innermost revelation of tragedy we always recognize ourselves as experienced strangers.) After that we shall have some necessary leisure to recover and to make the knowledge ours. The leisure will at first be brief and intense, hardly divided from the experience itself, but then slowing and widening as it moves more quietly into the dimension of time.

Old Manoa returns "With youthful steps," encouraged by his activity and the hope he has been begetting. He has been humiliating himself, as paternal reason was, before the Philistian Lords. The details come as a belated echo of our familiar recognition that Samson has now passed securely beyond this range of human consideration. The gap between Samson and the ordinary values of the world is displayed without new pressure on the hero, but as it were in retrospect. The account has an irrelevance that challenges nothing but offers a relaxed comedy of gratuitous contrast:

*"The Return of Samson." From* Heroic Knowledge: An Interpretation of *Paradise Regained* and *Samson Agonistes by Arnold Stein. (Minneapolis: University of Minnesota Press, 1957), pp. 192-202, 230-31 (notes). Copyright © 1957 by the University of Minnesota. Reprinted by permission of the publisher.*

> Others more moderate seeming, but thir aim
> Private reward, for which both God and State
> They easily would set to sale.

But the hated Philistia is divided into three parts, of which one part is humanly decent, "More generous far and civil," though no doubt well outnumbered by the business-minded third and the inflexible, religious-revengeful third.

Time has to be occupied until the big scene. Except for the punctuation of the two shouts, nothing new can happen, but old themes can be revived as a kind of mirror between past and future. Manoa and the Chorus discuss the role of fatherhood, now that Samson has reached the helplessness of old age before his father. Time is dealt with in a leisurely way, as if this reversal of normal order had somehow suspended time. The effect is not unlike a favorite one of Puccini's, the old pathos of hopefully planning ahead while the conductor fingers the page that will change those notes to tragic. Manoa's hope continues undaunted, but the effect is different. He does not stop with his paternal delight in tending Samson, but affirms his persuasion that God will "use him further yet in some great service,"

> And since his strength with eye-sight was not lost,
> God will restore him eye-sight to his strength.

There is prophetic ambiguity, of course, in the last phrase, but that is not the cause of the difference. Manoa has expressed the same kind of hope before: "His might continues in thee not for naught." The difference, I think, is less in Manoa than in the dramatic situation, though that perhaps allows us to see Manoa in a way not quite possible before, at least not without some straining. For one thing, Samson, after strenuous efforts befitting his tragic role, has moved closer to Manoa's hopefulness. The kind of enunciation that fitted the father before but jarred on the son now fits the son too. Even if this were not true, the absence of the hero grants Manoa's words a sincerity not clear before. He speaks his mind now, such as it is; there is no question of tempting the hero to patch things up glibly. Besides, we can see that his heart is not really in the idea of withdrawal. What he said before was the natural expression of his paternal care, but like Samson he believes in "use" and "service." The gap between them has to exist, for Samson is a tragic hero; but that gap is less wide than it seemed. Granted the necessary differences, Manoa can even manage to sound like Samson:

> Not to sit idle with so great a gift
> Useless, and thence ridiculous about him.

The "universal groan" accelerates time, but there are still ironic movements to be measured out. The Chorus assumes Manoa's familiar kind of hopefulness: what if Samson's eyesight has been miraculously restored? "Nothing is hard" to God. Manoa, hearing it said by someone else, hesitates: "That were a joy presumptuous to be thought." The Chorus presses him: God has performed miracles for His people before, "what hinders now?" Manoa has been saying that himself, but it is different when it comes from outside. He reminds one of Samson hoping for a retirement from the strife, until there is a specific proposal:

> He can I know, but doubt to think he will;
> Yet Hope would fain subscribe, and tempts Belief.

I pass by the set ironies of the first exchanges with the Messenger, and Manoa's lament, which brings to the surface the death-life theme more actively than since the beginning of the play. The big scene comes, after the deliberate small delays and after the deliberate large delay which is the whole drama. The presentation is formal and complete in itself. It gains tremendously, of course, from everything that has preceded and is now released; but it is worth noting that Milton has constructed the scene so that it can stand alone, independent and complete. If it had been published separately, or had been discovered in manuscript, we should regard it as an extraordinarily successful dramatic poem. One thing a conscious artist must have known before he wrote a word was how much would depend on the big scene, the only direct action in a moral drama of suffering developed through the indirect action of talk, and that talk filled with strenuous discriminations. It must have taken heroic self-confidence to choose the challenge, a mighty one, and then to endure the inevitable growth of the shadow as he approached the crucial moment with all the developed successes of the drama at stake, and quite able to fail. The technical answer—which will not explain the justified confidence of artistic genius—is to make the scene complete, to review at a final stage and on an elevated level the tragic mastery that has been nearly achieved.

We begin the scene from the distance already put between us and Samson, then approach him at the center of a new public stage, then return to him at the center of his old individual stage, and finally, perforce, step back to complete the cycle. First we have the Messenger's

point of view, which effectively creates a sense of the total scene, the
feeling of holiday and public triumph, beginning with sunrise and the
trumpeting announcement "Through each high street." The Messenger has normal human reactions, sorrow but curious desire to see.
He does not forget to describe the theater and its peculiar architecture;
he repeats the important detail of Samson's intermission, as realistic
fact overheard from those who stood nearer. The intoxicated mood and
atmosphere of triumph ("that insulting vanity") rises to a climax with
the entrance of Samson, seen as from a distance:

> The Feast and noon grew high, and Sacrifice
> Had fill'd thir hearts with mirth, high chear, & wine,
> When to thir sports they turn'd. Immediately
> Was *Samson* as a public servant brought,
> In thir state Livery clad; before him Pipes
> And Timbrels, on each side went armed guards,
> Both horse and foot before him and behind
> Archers, and Slingers, Cataphracts and Spears.
> At sight of him the people with a shout
> Rifted the Air clamouring thir god with praise,
> Who had made thir dreadful enemy thir thrall.

Then Samson is alone in the center of the stage, and we see him, as
from an indeterminate distance, in his new role of public entertainer:

> He patient but undaunted where they led him,
> Came to the place, and what was set before him
> Which without help of eye, might be assay'd,
> To heave, pull, draw, or break, he still perform'd
> All with incredible, stupendious force,
> None daring to appear Antagonist.

Here finally the ridicule is faced and mastered in a total victory of
patience. The internal anguish at folly, the writhing over the external
indignity—they have hindered him and they have helped him, but
now he is purged of his folly, for he has accepted it and the consequences entirely, followed it through to the end. He has been the
Athlete of God and failed. Now he is the Fool of God and succeeds.

We see what is happening and move toward him in our knowledge.
And then, at once, as he goes toward the pillars, we approach him more
closely than the hard strength of the man ever permitted, perhaps
more closely than his formidable weakness ever permitted.

> which when *Samson*
> Felt in his arms, with head a while enclin'd,
> And eyes fast fixt he stood, as one who pray'd,
> Or some great matter in his mind revolv'd.

This is the lover's touch he denied Dalila and was denied by Harapha. Now he has the "end" and the "use" in his arms, but it is not the old champion who is about to act. He has accepted his folly, possessed it, but not been possessed by it. He withdraws, in a gesture of wisdom learned through suffering. It is a brief gesture which would have profound significance even if the scene were an independent unit. But now we cannot fail to understand what he is doing, for the whole weight of the drama bears on the simple act, suspended as it is in a moment of complete silence on the last threshold. Even the presentation, from without, the objective reporting that carefully marks two possible interpretations of the external appearance, only heightens our sense of the inwardness of the simple gesture that sums up the play. He withdraws in thought and spirit before the final redemptive act which is to end the long process of redemption. He repeats, with a difference, the passive withdrawal from his true self which asserted the feminine pride of independence as a "petty god"; the passive withdrawal which mysteriously fulfilled itself by the "act" of passivity, the surrender to Dalila. The gesture recalls and acknowledges the sense of his human weakness and helplessness which assisted him against the temptations to withdraw in self-concern. But now he renews the admitted source of strength in God and marks the separation from self. For in this act of one revived hero against a nation there must be no shadow of individual pride. High point and low point confront each other again, as the grand motion completes itself and the inspired end comes to meet him.

The released spirit trumpets the announcement as preface to the deed:

> At last with head erect thus cryed aloud,
> Hitherto, Lords, what your commands impos'd
> I have perform'd, as reason was, obeying,
> Not without wonder or delight beheld.
> Now of my own accord such other tryal
> I mean to shew you of my strength, yet greater;
> As with amaze shall strike all who behold.

The weakness of Samson, which has been defined by moral and intellectual strength, is at last granted the expression of strength. The saint's victory over himself through patience becomes, through the inspired "command from Heav'n," the champion's triumphant recovery of his "end." The accomplishment is gift, as plainly as the first gift of superhuman strength, but now the gift has been earned through human means, so that we are able to identify ourselves with Samson and the expression of his achieved recovery just as the gift turns authentically tragic, to death. That ensures our proper human relationship to the superhuman gift. To see what has happened, we have only to think of the first choral celebration of his strength. That was magnificent, and credible, but it had between us and it the distance of irrevocable history, and the very magnificence of the rhetoric consciously re-creating what no longer existed. Now all the distance is between the *inspired* Samson (with all he has come to represent) and the Philistines. He commands the knowledge and the voice of a prophet, marking for others the folly of ignorance, as he has, with the help of others, marked it for himself.

We begin to move backward from the height of the shock, our feelings expressed for us and guided through several stages. The Messenger initiates the movement by the exultation that begins to creep into his description of the result. The first choral reaction welcomes the victory, but with no notable release of feeling until after three main facts are named: Samson's fulfillment of his "work," the nature of the death (not suicide), and the dimension of the victory.

The Semichorus takes up this last item, involving national passion as it does, and releases the first and deepest wave of human feeling—hate. It is a fierce chant of triumph; all the ridicule endured by Samson is turned against the enemy in one unsparing recital of the ignorance which is folly:

> While thir hearts were jocund and sublime,
> Drunk with Idolatry, drunk with Wine,
> And fat regorg'd of Bulls and Goats,
> Chaunting thir Idol, and preferring
> Before our living Dread who dwells
> In *Silo* his bright Sanctuary:
> Among them he a spirit of phrenzie sent,
> Who hurt thir minds,
> And urg'd them on with mad desire
> To call in hast for thir destroyer;

> They only set on sport and play
> Unweetingly importun'd
> Thir own destruction to come speedy upon them.
> So fond are mortal men
> Fall'n into wrath divine,
> As thir own ruin on themselves to invite,
> Insensate left, or to sense reprobate,
> And with blindness internal struck.

This is more than "comely" and "reviving." The celebration of divine justice and of the self-destruction of evil comes as a full purge of doubts and fears.

The second Semichorus moves from the primitive to a more "civilized" range of feeling. It begins with direct exultation in the hero and a contrasting contempt for the enemy (hate is no longer appropriate). It turns finally with fuller attention to the return of the hero, celebrated now not to express human hate but hope:

> But he though blind of sight,
> Despis'd and thought extinguish't quite,
> With inward eyes illuminated
> His fierie vertue rouz'd
> From under ashes into sudden flame,
> And as an ev'ning Dragon came,
> Assailant on the perched roosts,
> And nests in order rang'd
> Of tame villatic Fowl; but as an Eagle
> His cloudless thunder bolted on thir heads.
> So vertue giv'n for lost,
> Deprest, and overthrown, as seem'd,
> Like that self-begott'n bird
> In the *Arabian* woods embost,
> That no second knows nor third,
> And lay e're while a Holocaust,
> From out her ashie womb now teem'd,
> Revives, reflourishes, then vigorous most
> When most unactive deem'd,
> And though her body die, her fame survives,
> A secular bird ages of lives.

Manoa takes us one further stage away from the height of action. The Philistines are spoken of without either hate or contempt. National joy is revised into the challenging opportunity for freedom, if Israel finds courage "to lay hold on this occasion." The expression of human hope celebrated in the return of the hero is carried toward its conclusion as the tragic experience closes the gap between the hero and his people, through the "best and happiest" realization that God was "not parted from him, as was feard." And Manoa's optimism, so dissonant early in the play, is granted the high privilege of the purged human response to Samson's tragedy:

> Nothing is here for tears, nothing to wail
> Or knock the breast, no weakness, no contempt,
> Dispraise, or blame, nothing but well and fair,
> And what may quiet us in a death so noble.

At the height of the action there are three distinguishable sacrifices. These we may consider as ritualistic,[1] both from the perspective of a modern concept of tragedy and from the authoritative response of the audience. First, there is the regular course of sacrifice (off stage, as it were) of the Philistine festival, leading to the high point of the public enjoyment of Samson, which marks the drunken Philistine height of noon and turns the frenzied sacrificers into sacrifice. It is this second sacrifice that the first Semichorus celebrates in its ritualistic triumph, and catharsis, of hate. In that terrible chant Samson is only the instrument created by Philistine ignorance. The third sacrifice is Samson, and as the audience responds to the event the nature of the sacrifice may be seen to evolve. The first stage is the primitive release of animal fear from the lowest human depths. The second stage elevates the hero from being a mere instrument of the Philistine's brutal ignorance and hate to being a symbol of human hope and virtue. Finally, he is united to his people and their religion by the noble death which "may quiet us." There is a still further stage in the ritualizing of the sacrifice, but before I come to that I want to quote, for its relevance to Samson's case, a striking conclusion from Gertrude R. Levy's remarkable book, *The Gate of Horn*. She is considering Pythagoras after having studied certain anticipatory patterns in primitive religion:

> His discipline was still the 'Way of Death,' and his ritual sacrifice; but now the animal victim existed only within the soul, a force to be liberated for creation, as the bull's blood had been poured out long ago. It did not involve a rejection of the life of the senses, but an absorption of power by their control, as it did for Plato after him.[2]

[1] For some interesting comments, from a Burkean point of view, on ritualistic death in *Samson Agonistes,* see Kenneth Burke, *A Rhetoric of Motives* (New York: Prentice-Hall, 1950), pp. 3-10, 16-17, 19.

[2] (London: Faber and Faber, 1948), p. 308. If Levy's point drawn as it is from

This has some bearing on Samson's sacrifice. I remind the reader of the debt Samson's redemption owes, from the beginning, to his capacity for feeling. Though he subdues the raw immediacies of feeling into a more noble temper, he does not stifle, or reject, or eradicate: he sacrifices. The powers of intellect, justice, patience—these are helped in this tragedy by the burning sense of the necessary "animal" self. I shall not review my scattered observations. I point only to the sustained theme of ridicule, over which Samson agonizes, but which assists him time and again: as at the last moment with Dalila; and with the Messenger, as the hero proceeds to the feast, not trailed through the streets "like a wild Beast," but "as reason was"; and as he performs the penultimate sacrifice by mastering, as the patient Fool of God, the final consequences of his folly.

Finally, the austere poet who could deal so sternly with the fate of the Garden of Eden allows a human dignity to ritual and place. The Samson who becomes a symbol of human hope and virtue also becomes a mere person, and there is a dead body to be cleansed and buried with proper ceremony. Decorum, both human and poetic, requires the ritual. The return of Samson to God is a return to his people, and they must, since this tragedy *is* a shared experience, not walk away numb and dumb. They need this expression of human decency and dignity, to mark the return of Samson to them and to mark their return, through the shared experience, closer to the God Whose "faithful Champion" Samson has "in the close" proved to be.

But the ritual goes beyond the bounds of simple communal decency and relationship. There is a monument, a shrine, to be built, not en-

---

an insight of modern anthropology, seems too sophisticated to explain a seventeenth-century poem, I can defend it from some of Milton's own cultural background. As a humanist he never completely subscribes to one extreme biblical (and Stoic and Neoplatonic) view, that the will and passions are to be not mastered but entirely rooted out. As Cassirer justly says (*The Platonic Renaissance in England*, p. 107): "Erasmus sees the goal of Christianity, not in the suppression and destruction of the human will, but in the education, the 'discipline of the will.'" Or as my lord Ottaviano says in Castiglione's *The Book of the Courtier* (Book IV, 18): "I did not say that temperance wholly removes and uproots the passions from the human mind, nor would it be well to do this, for even the passions contain some elements of good; but it reduces to the sway of reason that which is perverse in our passions and recusant to right. Therefore it is not well to extirpate the passions altogether; for this would be like making an edict that no man must drink wine, in order to be rid of drunkenness. . . . Thus, when moderated by temperance, the passions are helpful to virtue, like the wrath that aids strength, hatred of evil-doers aids justice, and likewise the other virtues are aided by the passions; which, if they were wholly removed, would leave the reason very weak and languid. . . . Nor is this less true of justice."

tirely unlike shrines built by the pagan world for its heroes (as Hercules). It is true that Samson is not to be "worshipped" as the hero of
a pagan cult, or as the saint of an "idolatrous" Christian practice. Samson will serve as national inspiration to the "valiant youth"; to the
Hebrew virgins (as to Christian homiletics) he will serve as moral example; what else he will mean to the virgins we are left the not-dif-
ficult task of interpreting. But still, Milton is here poetically sanction-
ing a shrine. Even if we knew nothing of the man beyond the compass
of this poem, we should still recall with surprise that Samson's tomb re-
sembles the one Dalila prophesied for herself, also to be visited with
"annual flowers," and her acts were also to be recorded in song. Is
Milton belatedly recognizing and dignifying a basic human urge?—
one that could turn a grave allegedly Milton's into a ritual of shared
experience for souvenir hunters!

Our best answer to the surprising extension of ritual is, I think, to
be found in the decorum which maintains the inner truth of the drama.
That decorum has not faltered in expressing any necessary extreme of
feeling. There is no hesitation now. The hero has returned to the community, on his own terms. Heroic and ordinary morality have come
together, but not quite together. The "true experience" of the tragedy
still is individual, commonly available and elevating to the community,
but not quite as a common, institutionalized moral property. There is
no authorized identification of the two orders of morality, as in the
Philistine "public good." The height of the "true experience" now
can afford, without danger, some inadequate translation into the terms
of the community. The "valiant youth" will not finally distort, for
theirs is not the most adequate, nor the last, word. And this is equally
true of the virgins and their humor of no humor:

> only bewailing
> His lot unfortunate in nuptial choice,
> From whence captivity and loss of eyes.

There is a still larger community, for whom the truth of Samson's
tragic experience is individual and transcends both local place and
time. It is to this community that the Chorus addresses its last word,
"All is best, though we oft doubt." The tragedy has exercised human
doubt fully and deeply, in order to serve the moral and intellectual
purpose of spreading doubt thin.[3] Socratic catharsis of ignorance joins
Aristotelian catharsis of passion in the drama of knowledge:

[3] I think I have been remembering here some notable words of F. H. Bradley

His servants he with new acquist
Of true experience from this great event
With peace and consolation hath dismist,
And calm of mind all passion spent.

---

*(Essays on Truth and Reality* [Oxford: Clarendon Press, 1914], pp. 17f): "But in philosophy, so far as philosophy succeeds . . . doubt here is not smothered or expelled but itself is assimilated and used up. . . . A scepticism that has tried to be thorough tends, we may say, to weaken doubt by spreading it and making it more general. The doubt, if really it is intellectual and not a mere disease of the will, loses strength and loses terror by losing its contrast."

One final note on the gap between individual and social morality. For all Martin Buber's heroic and admirable modern effort to relate the religious ethos to the body politic, his underlying moral position is founded on the morality of the individual soul. He uses the theological resources imaginatively, but some of his bridgework one may sympathize with more than one may approve. His political hero is willingly "bound" to the body politic, and cannot remain aloof, though he does not abandon himself blindly "to any of its movements, rather confronting each movement watchfully and carefully that it does not miss truth and loyalty." His great goal is to change the crowd into individuals. "And if he does not achieve much he has time, he has God's own time." See *Between Man and Man*, tr. R. G. Smith (Boston: Beacon Press, 1955), pp. 64f

# Structural and Doctrinal Pattern in
# Milton's Later Poems: *Samson Agon istes*[1]

## *by Arthur E. Barker*

### *I*

The doctrine of Christian liberty which Professor Woodhouse has shown to be of such crucial significance in Milton's prose, as in radical Puritan revolutionary theory,[2] serves as a focus for Milton's developing preoccupations and might provide interpreters with a further means

"*Structural and Doctrinal Pattern in Milton's Later Poems:* Samson Agonistes," *by Arthur E. Barker. From* Essays in English Literature from the Renaissance to the Victorian Age presented to A.S.P. Woodhouse, *eds. Miller MacLure and F. W. Watt. (Toronto: University of Toronto Press, 1964), pp. 172-79. Copyright © 1964 by Toronto University Press. Reprinted by permission of the author and publisher.*

[1] This essay forms part of a study, too long to be published in this volume, in which the application of the doctrine of Christian liberty to Milton's later poems is preceded by an extensive interpretation of the public prose and of the implications of the revisions to *De Doctrina Christiana* in their bearing on my central argument, here replaced (as section I) by a short summary [which has been here further abridged—ED.].

[2] "Puritanism and Liberty," *University of Toronto Quarterly*, IV (1934-5), 395-404; "Milton, Puritanism and Liberty, *UTQ*, IV (1934-5), 483-513, especially 487, note 7; "Puritanism and Democracy," *Canadian Journal of Economics and Political Science*, IV (1938), 1-21; *Puritanism and Liberty* (London, 1938); review of Haller, *Rise of Puritanism, American Historical Review*, XLV (1945), 123-5; "Background for Milton," *UTQ*, X (1940-1), 499-505; "Seventeenth-Century Radicals," *UTQ*, XV (1945-6), 98-101; "Religion and Some Foundations of English Democracy," *Philosophical Review*, LXI (1952), 503-31; *Milton the Poet* (Toronto, 1955), 12.

Subsequent references to these studies are by title and page. Where no author is indicated for other items, the author is Professor Woodhouse, save for bracketed references for Milton in the text, to volume and page of *Works* (Columbia), unless otherwise indicated in notes. The omission of acknowledgments of debts to other authorities (which students will easily recognize as requiring throughout heavy annotation) may be forgiven and postponed to another occasion, in favor of an effort to acknowledge, to such extent as is at least indicatively possible, the debts demanding appropriate recognition on this occasion, among which, as some readers will be aware and others will readily perceive, must be counted the accumulation of unof clarifying the cruxes of his later poems. Though the phrase does not occur in the poems, and though scholarship rightly associates the doctrine chiefly with the radical Miltonic assertions of "private or domestic liberty" and liberty of conscience, its revolutionary Miltonic development, with its associated complex of doctrines, and the centrality of these for both books of *De Doctrina Christiana,* may suggest the possibility of its having contributed significantly to the structure of the later poems and the terms out of which their representation of experience develops its meaning. . . .

The poetic significance of Milton's developing notions about the process of regeneration on which Christian liberty depends for him is not obscured but underlined by our interest in the historical (or modern) bearing of his revolutionary arguments and our interest in his handling of doctrines of less obviously immediate experiential significance which, however, ultimately serve only as buttresses for orientations of this focal problem. Most of what he wrote, consciously or unconsciously, ironically or naïvely, points to the matter, so that, as Professor Woodhouse has said,[3] he seems always to be making his way, through whatever lapses, deluges, or thickets, towards the later poems. The extant revisions and additions made in the manuscript of *De Doctrina* all focus attention on his preoccupation with redemption and the process of regeneration and the Christian liberty resulting from the process; the most obvious clusters of revisions occur in the chapters on Christ's mediatorial office, on man's "natural renovation" and "calling," on his "supernatural renovation" and "regeneration" and "being planted in Christ," on the Covenant of Grace, including Law and Gospel, on Christian liberty. "Natural" renovation is the process through which God invites all men to a knowledge of true propitiation and worship, a calling which includes such as have never heard of Christ, since they are called through what they can know of God, if they will, simply from his creation, though their responsive faith in God is made possible by the redeeming Christ they know not (XV, 344, 346-8, 403-5). "Regeneration" is the effect of the "supernatural renovation" which follows a willing and believing response to calling with the repentance that this must induce; it extends the proc-

---

identifiable debts of many years of close relation—going back indeed to undergraduate inability to attempt an answer to the question, on an examination set by Professor Woodhouse in 1932, as to whether Milton should be thought a Puritan or a Christian rationalist.

[3] "Milton and his Readers," *UTQ,* XVIII (1948-9), 204; *Milton the Poet,* 13; "The Argument of *Paradise Lost,*" *UTQ,* XVI (1946-7), 435.

ess of natural renovation which cannot be extended without it. What supernatural renovation restores, in men who exercise their responsibility, their naturally renovated and their new powers thus to obtain salvation, is the divine image. Milton was never moved to revise his belief that the unwritten Law of God is that "law of nature" given to the first man, of which remnants and a kind of reflection remain in all men's hearts, and which in the regenerate is day by day being renovated in the direction of its primitive (or prelapsarian) perfection. But his continuing concern for the Christian liberty related to it is evidenced by revisions which stress the abrogation of the whole Mosaic Law by the Gospel to emphasize the law in the renovated heart as the basis of true liberty, and this in turn depends upon what Milton thinks the demonstrable continuity of a providence which makes possible similar responsibilities and opportunities under every dispensation, not only under the prelapsarian and Christian but under all dispensations (with their appropriate differences) in between. What God consistently gives his responsive creatures is an opportunity to respond to his providential processes—and to all creatures his own good time. Towards this the most significant revisions of *De Doctrina* are making their way.

## II

Milton's later poems elaborate and represent his notions about the process of regeneration by filling in, mimetically, what *De Doctrina* leaves confused, its operation even under pre-Christian dispensations. Whatever the poems may do with the treatise's heresies about the Son, Creation, and so on,[4] the function of these remains—what it was in

---

[4] Nothing in Milton is, in the end, "indifferent" or "peripheral" to his main theme; but there are limits to such percipience and comprehension as ordinary readers can muster in response, and the relations of his "major" heresies to his theme demand special knowledge. See "Notes on Milton's Views on the Creation: The Initial Phase," *Philological Quarterly*, XXVIII (1949), where what is perhaps of most immediate relevance to the point in hand would seem to be, 227-8, the "neutral" yet "potential" quality of the first, far-from-nought matter (cf. "Pattern in *Paradise Lost*," *UTQ*, XXII [1952-3], 124)—though through the Satanic eye it seems simply disordered rather than "unordered," and especially Milton's insistence on the "voluntary" (if also rational) creative act, 213-14, on the "dregs" to be purged away and the problem of evil, 229-30, and on "potentiality," 223-4, 234. See the recent articles by W. B. Hunter, especially "Milton's Arianism Reconsidered," *Harvard Theological Review*, LII (1959), 9-35, on the Son, especially on the theories of "subordinationism" and the Son's participation in the Father's will and of "pre-

the treatise—the buttressing of the conviction that God's accommodating ways to men, as they are illuminated in Scripture and however wrathfully left-handed they may seem to the unresponsive, are manifested in the demanding and sustaining process of responsive individual natural and supernatural experience as it develops in time. The poems use, without any substantial change whatever and indeed in literally prolonging echoes, all the doctrines to which the manuscript revisions call attention. In general they use the doctrines focusing on the incompleteness of earlier dispensations and the consequent appearance of discontinuity between successive dispensations to provide the poems with their structural patterns and circumstantial details; but the development of the mimetic action depends on the implications of the doctrines and revisions concerned with response to the developing continuity of God's ways through all dispensations. "Christian liberty" nowhere appears in the later poems, not simply because the exhaustion of frustrated controversy has wearied Milton with the spectrum of the seventeenth century's confused and futile fragmentation of it, but because decorum and theology alike render it inappropriate in the representation of experience under pre-Christian dispensations. Yet "Christian liberty" is what the poems are about. Their aim indeed is to re-focus the fragmented bands of the spectrum in a unified ray, illuminating any individual's experience, by inducing seventeenth-century Christian readers to realize the point of God's continuous ways by mimetic participation in the responses or failures of response of other men (or indeed of angels, since all creatures are involved) to their process, as it manifested itself in the circumstantially contrasting but essentially and developingly related conditions of other dispensations, and as these point towards the clarifications of responsibility available to Christians because they all involve covenants progressively, though adequately enough for what their times demand, implying the New Covenant (as it implies its own ultimate fulfilment).

Since God's ways to men (or angels) are continuously constant but developing, the essentials of the response demanded remain constant but essentially imply their continuous development, from one dispensation to another, from one segment of individual experience to an-

---

dominance" and the union of the two wills in Christ (with implications for both the married relation and the church inviting the expectation of significant elaboration). Such discernible revisions in the manuscript as bear on these matters would seem to relate them to the process of renovation. Here I have to record my debt to the work in progress of my research assistants, Mr. Lindsay A. Mann and Miss Mary Elizabeth Merril, of Champaign-Urbana.

other. On the one hand is the universal process of God's ways; on the other the process of individual experience which fulfils itself in the degree to which it corresponds with God's ways as they manifest themselves in successive dispensations. Hence the terms of the poems are the developing structure of universal history and the individual's response to experience. Though at first sight recent English history seems to be frustratedly excluded, it is of course not so. The licenser was rightly troubled by his perception at least of the tail of the comet that fills kings with fear when they hear the Gospel speaking much of liberty. The echoes of the prose in the diatribes against tyrants, hirelings, women, by Samson's chorus, the young Christ, Michael—who is of course very precisely summarizing for his immediate purposes the conclusions of the frustrated political prose and especially the tracts of 1659 on conscience—established a relation between the prose and the poems and set the pattern of recent irresponsible history very firmly, by something more than implication, in its place in the apparently universal pattern of the degenerate beat of tyrannical and anarchical history. But the rhythm which contains this beat is, for Milton, really universal; and this is chiefly recognizable, in the clear light of the comet's body, through the corresponding rhythm of responsive individual experience, thrown into relief by irresponsible contrast. Hence the focus of the poems is on the individual (though by no means in isolation); and their systematic theology and transcendent vision are used in the representation of the psychology of what Milton thinks true religious experience under any dispensation—a subject experience had evidently taught him, with others in his period, to think Protestantism very much needed to include in its curriculum since its tendency, however initially humble or despairing, to ascribe all responsibility to God's secret will and pleasure had had such confusing consequences. As the Christian dispensation fulfils, though by discontinuous continuity, earlier dispensations, so Christian liberty depends on a response which fulfils, and not simply by contrast, the responses demanded by earlier dispensations. The response the mimesis invites from its seventeenth-century reader is not simply an analogous response. Rightly or wrongly, Milton does not segregate his theory of poetry and its function from his theory of the process of regeneration or his view of religious experience or irreligious experience. As his prose parallels and prefatory comments indicate, Aristotelean Italianate words like "katharsis" or "decorum" always imply for him their meaning in the context of the regenerative process as his northern mind understands it, since poetry is an imitation of this accommodatingly purgative and illuminating art of God. Indeed, the "literal" is opposed to the "literary" and the "poetic" and the recognition of this, or failure to recognize it, is part of the process of experience represented by the mimesis. In the process of the response it invites, image and meaning become inseparable, as do genre and meaning,[5] for he is not using pagan images or classical genre to convey a simply contrasting Christian theme: as he thinks the classical genres, when they were well used, the product of a developing response to the law of nature to which a supernatural dimension is added by the corresponding prophetic and poetical parts of Scripture, so he thinks the Christian theme fulfils what was truly responsive in the classical. Since, as *De Doctrina* says (XV, 199), all acts are good and evil is only obliquity and anomaly in terms of the right direction it thus illuminates, the obliquities and anomalies of actions under other dispensations only serve to illustrate the direction to be more clearly revealed by the Gospel, by which, according to *recta ratio,* Christians are required to bring into action the natural and supernatural gifts of the Spirit, pregnantly working in all dispensations.

Thus Milton's late (and somewhat ambiguously espoused) companion pieces both depend, for their doctrinal significance, their circumstantial decorum, their sustaining structure and development, not simply on the everywhere implied contrast and relation between Christian liberty's Gospel and the Old Dispensation but on the contrast and relation between the Law and the Prophets.[6] Samson's experience is so far from having no middle that it is in effect all middle, as Judges, following after Law, in the Chronicles of time from giants onward, must imply the poetical and prophetic to follow; and the process of his response to experience thus leads him from the childhood of law

[5] "Pattern in *Paradise Lost,*" *UTQ,* XXII (1952-3), 109, 114; "Tragic Effect in *Samson Agonistes,*" *UTQ,* XXVIII (1958-9), 205; "Some Reflections on How to Read Milton," *Seventeenth-Century News,* XVI (1958), 8-9.

[6] The question of the dating of the composition of *Samson* must here be ignored, as chiefly, in the absence of documentation, a question of "internal evidence" and hence "interpretation": Woodhouse, "Historical Criticism," *Publications of the Modern Language Association,* LXVI (1951), 1063; "Samson Agonistes and Milton's Experience," *Transactions of the Royal Society of Canada,* Series III, vol. XLIII (1949), Sec. 2, 157-60; *Milton the Poet,* 14. It must suffice to express the impression that, whenever the poem was *begun,* it was "finished" (no doubt like the "undergraduate" and "graduate" academic exercises and many other of Milton's writings) just before it was sent (late) to the printer—and indeed perhaps (as in other cases) just before the presses stopped printing. Doctrinal and emotional differences between the companion pieces remain a matter of free opinion; but at least *PR,* 639 and *SA,* 1733 and their contexts are related in the right order.

and its despairing uncertainty, resulting from apparent failure, to a recognition of what the Law underlines through failure: the real significance of the original call to the use of natural powers in merely national and physical heroism. It is not simply Samson's suicidal fulfilment of himself in the end as vista-vision national folk-hero that gives the mimesis its significance but what this doubly retributive fulfilment after failure implies. This implication is underlined by Samson's special Nazarite concern for the requirements of the Law, which itself is underlined by the Old Testament preoccupations and difficulties of the chorus of Ebrewes. The point for everybody is that his failure and despair, as impinged on by the incidents of the poem, lead him to recognize God's constantly renovating calling and to respond in a way which further contradicts and undermines the dictates of the Law yet indicates its fulfilment and the significance of his earlier "national" callings and failures. Whether or not Milton had or had not any higher-critical awareness of the stratifications in the version of the story in Judges, of its naturalistic Paul-Bunyanesque origins, its elaboration in terms of God's Law for and covenant with his chosen people in whatever Dead-Sea scrolls, and its prophetic overtones, he was certainly aware that the aim of conflicting patristic and later commentary was to get out of the story the full implications of what the author of the Epistle to the Hebrews saw in it—and in comparable illegal actions by other Old Testament heroes, such as a favorite of the prose, David and the shew-bread. Milton's manipulation of the story in terms of the percipient Greek tragic genre[7] (or more percipient Revelation) organizes it to induce the katharsis and the illumination involved in such actions in an audience which rightly sees Samson as a Hebraic Hercules but whose humanism is inclined to read him back down below the level of insight attained even by Greek tragedy or nationalism. The best gloss we have on this manipulation and on Milton's prefatory expressions of opinion about the use and implication of Greek tragic convention (and its limitations), may be found in *De Doctrina's* chapters on calling and renovation, repentance and faith, and their sustaining extension in supernatural renovation towards Christian liberty. These suggest, especially as to Law and Gospel, that the strictly preserved Greek and, what is more important, Hebraic decorum of the piece—underlined by the chorus which is, if nothing else, in every way decorous—is designed to focus on the progressively

---

[7] "Tragic Effect in *Samson Agonistes*," *UTQ*, XXVIII (1958-9), 205.

realized fact that it is not Samson's resistance to the repetition of temptations alone (triple or otherwise)[8] that is of primary importance but what makes this negative resistance possible, his progressive response to the renewed calling of the renovation of his natural powers and thence his awareness of new faculties that, as Hebraic Hercules, he stupidly never dreamed he potentially had—until he recognizes that his real strength was never in his hair but in the living God and that all his actions have been perverse and inadequate parodies of the significance of his calling, as his sacrifice of his hair and natural power to love of Dalila was a parody of another kind of sacrifice, which he might, even in domestic relations with an unbeliever, have better imitated. Hence his being led to something extraordinary under the Law, like the other figures cited by Hebrews and *De Doctrina*.

Each of Samson's temptations is itself a parody related to the Law and containing distorted elements of the truth of what is really demanded under the Law. They reminiscentially underline, ironically, the increasingly parodic quality of Samson's own earlier acts, chiefly motivated by the impercipient preoccupation with his function as national hero and his own natural strength which made him his own idol. Hence Manoa's well-intentioned but senile offer of juvenile ransom, the braggart parody of Harapha's challenge, and even more centrally Dalila's apologetic parody of deeds answerable to a loyalty higher than the merely patriotic. The process of Samson's fumbling but repentant response to the implications of these parodies—which causes the choral commentators so much uneasiness—marks the stages in the renovating movement out of despair and beyond the Law. The process is marked by, among other things, the changes in Samson's tone of voice which become most complex at the center, in response to Dalila, blending other notes with indignation in a way perplexing to both severity and sentiment. The double-scened "act" that follows indicates that the righteous indignation that must greet Harapha is not inconsistent with the quite uncharacteristic gentleness—though there was the boy—of the effort to reassure the beaten chorus of the ultimate

[8] Review of Krouse, *Milton's Samson, Modern Language Notes*, LXVI (1951), 118, for the traditional view that the moral center of interest, in Samson's sin and repentance is incompatible with the prophetic emphasis on him as a "type" of Christ; "Samson Agonistes and Milton's Experience," *Transactions of the Royal Society of Canada*, Series III, vol. XLIII (1949), Sec. 2, 162-72, for *Samson* as "a study in regeneration," and "Tragic Effect in *Samson Agonistes*," *UTQ*, XXVIII (1958-9), 206-7, 213, on freedom of will and God's providence.

rightness, despite the apparent repetition of obliquity, of the culminating action to which he is being called.

Such reassurance is not easy to induce or come by, for uneasy
poetical messengers and their audiences. It perhaps can only be
achieved, each for himself after what support others have intentionally
or unintentionally provided, in such moments as that in which, as we
hear, Samson stands alone and waiting, with head bowed and arms
outstretched between two stony pillars. One of the striking (and
evidently self-restrained) effects of the later poems is that they move
towards such moments of silence, in which the reader is left to decide,
in terms of his response to the controlled mimetic movement, what is
happening and is meant. Manoa and the Hebrew chorus do not quite
tell us the meaning, but only that the moment is to be remembered
and the meaning of its new aquist sought after the event.

If the movement and the moment may be glossed in terms of *De
Doctrina*'s renovation towards Christian liberty, this does not mean
that Samson possessed "Christian liberty," or that he is, without important distinctions and reservations, a "type" of Christ or even of
the Christian. He cannot possess Christian liberty, by definition, because he is acting under the as-yet-unabrogated dispensation of the
Law, the demands of whose decorum must be preserved at whatever
sacrifice, since they may provide a fulcrum for some though a stum-
bling stone to others. As a revision in the manuscript of *De Doctrina*
observes, under the Law those who trusted in God were justified by
faith "but not without the works of the Law" (XVI, 150). So Manoa;
if with limited and even neo-classical percipience. But the implication
of the spirit in which in his time Samson fulfils himself and the Law
requires further comment. A type is significant both for its contrast
with and its likeness to what it types, by being itself according to the
decorum of the circumstances of its dispensation in time and an indication of what the process of time moves towards. As to human individuals or types, despite frustration, Milton never lost his conviction
that the fulfilment of the particular is the end of the experiential
process, not its being swallowed up in some vaguely indefinable over-
soul of meaning. In his way and time, Samson is the type of what
the Christian may be the type of in his way and time, fulfilling the
letter of the type by bringing into appropriate action the gifts of the
Spirit. Even the typical destruction of temples or rebuilding of them
appropriate to one dispensation may prove inappropriate to another;

but the spirit of the type continues to fulfil itself, appropriately to God's secular ways, in time. Hence the chorus: with its culminating implications at least of the Prophets, perhaps even of the Epistle to the Hebrews. . . .

# From Shadowy Types to Truth

## by *William G. Madsen*

The key to an understanding of *Samson Agonistes* is the method of biblical interpretation known as typology. In its narrowest sense the theory of typology states that certain persons, things, and events of the Old Testament are symbolic prefigurations, foreshadowings, or types of certain persons, things, and events of the New Testament. Thus Joshua is a type of Christ (the antitype); the synagogue a type of the Christian church; the sacrifice of Isaac a type of the Crucifixion. Sometimes the antitypes are not limited to the New Testament but extended to the whole Christian church and its members. The exodus of the Jews from Egypt to the Promised Land may be regarded (as it was by Dante) as a type of the journey of every Christian soul from the fleshpots of this world through the wilderness of self-denial and suffering to the Promised Land of Heaven. Some theologians have regarded certain persons and events of the New Testament as types whose antitypes are to be found in the future history of the Church. The method can even be extended beyond the confines of the Bible to encompass pagan history and literature. Dante regarded the Roman Empire as a foreshadowing of the Catholic Church, and Renaissance Neoplatonists were fond of seeing in Hercules a type of Christ and in pagan sacrifices a foreshadowing of the Mass.

Typological interpretation of the Old Testament was universally practiced by both Protestants and Catholics in Milton's day, and it fell into disuse only in the eighteenth and nineteenth centuries. It has recently enjoyed a revival among theologians, although there is nothing like general agreement about how it is to be applied or even about its general validity as a mode of interpretation. Some modern theologians reject it altogether; others would limit the Old Testament

*"From Shadowy Types to Truth," by William G. Madsen. From* The Lyric and Dramatic Milton: Selected Papers from the English Institute, *ed. Joseph H. Summers. (New York: Columbia University Press, 1965), pp. 95-114. Copyright © 1965 by Columbia University Press. Reprinted by permission of the publisher. Introductory remarks outlining recent critical opinion concerning the Christian spirit of* Samson Agonistes *have been omitted—*Ed.

types to those explicitly mentioned in the New Testament; a minority
feel free to exercise their own critical judgment or ingenuity. We need
not concern ourselves here with the technical rules for discovering
types laid down by theologians. The following observations, derived
from a study of the types commonly accepted by Milton's contemporaries, will be sufficient for our merely literary purpose:

1. A type is a historical person or event, not a mythical person or a
recurrent event like the rising and setting of the sun.

2. A type looks forward in time, not upward through the scale of
being. The theory of typology is thus firmly grounded in the Judaeo-
Christian world of existences and is fundamentally alien to the Greek
world of essences.

3. Natural objects may be types, but they are usually such only in
special historical circumstances. St. Paul tells us that the rock that
Moses struck was Christ (the water that issued forth was regarded as
a type of the blood and water that flowed from Christ's side when it
was pierced by the spear); this does not mean that every rock is a type
of Christ.

4. There must be differences as well as similarities between a type
and its antitype. (A most important rule for *Samson,* as we shall see.)

5. Neither the actors of a typical event nor the authors of their
history understand the typological significance of what they are doing
or writing. The Jews wandering in the wilderness did not know that
manna prefigured the Eucharist, nor did Joshua know that in leading
his people into the Promised Land he was a type of Jesus leading his
people into Heaven.

6. Hence, the meaning of a type cannot be known until it has been
fulfilled in its antitype.

Although Milton is often credited with a strictly rationalistic theory
of biblical interpretation, references to the doctrine of typology may
be found in writings from all periods of his life. In *The Reason of
Church Government* he says that "all those sumptuous things under
the law, were made to signify the inward beauty and splendor of the
Christian church," and he draws an elaborate analogy between the new
temple described in the prophecy of Ezekiel and the soul of man,
which is God's "rational temple." [1] In *Paradise Lost* Michael explains
the significance of the Law to Adam in these words:

---

[1] *The Reason of Church Government,* I.ii, in *John Milton: Complete Poems and
Major Prose,* ed. Merritt Y. Hughes (New York: Odyssey Press, 1957), pp. 645-6. All
quotations from Milton are taken from this edition.

> So Law appears imperfet, and but giv'n
> With purpose to resign them in full time
> Up to a better Cov'nant, disciplin'd
> From shadowy Types to Truth, from Flesh to Spirit,
> From imposition of strict Laws, to free
> Acceptance of large Grace, from servile fear
> To filial, works of Law to works of Faith. (XII.300-306)

What has this to do with Samson? Critics as different in their assumptions and methods as Hanford, Krouse, and Woodhouse agree that Milton did not present Samson as a type of Christ. It is true, of course, that there are no explicit references to Samson as a type of Christ. How could there be when the words of the drama are confined to Old Testament actors? The meaning of a type cannot be known until the antitype has been revealed, and Samson and Manoa and the Chorus know nothing of Christ. That there are, in fact, implicit foreshadowings of Christ in Milton's Samson I shall suggest in a moment; perhaps it is even more important for an understanding of Milton's conception of Samson, however, to recognize the differences between them, for it is essential to the whole doctrine of typology that the type be different from as well as similar to the antitype.

The major differences between Samson and the Christ of *Paradise Regained* can be summed up as action vs. passion and letter (or flesh) vs. spirit (or word).

Just after Harapha leaves, the Chorus exults in the return of Samson's heroic vigor:

> Oh how comely it is and how reviving
> To the Spirits of just men long opprest!
> When God into the hands of thir deliverer
> Puts invincible might
> To quell the mighty of the Earth, th' oppressor,
> The brute and boist'rous force of violent men
> Hardy and industrious to support
> Tyrannic power, but raging to pursue
> The righteous and all such as honor Truth. (1268-76)

Mindful of Samson's plight, however, the Chorus goes on to suggest that his vocation may be that of the patient sufferer:

> But patience is more oft the exercise
> Of Saints, the trial of thir fortitude,
> Making them each his own Deliverer,

> And Victor over all
> That tyranny or fortune can inflict.
> Either of these is in thy lot,
> *Samson,* with might endu'd
> Above the Sons of men; but sight bereav'd
> May chance to number thee with those
> Whom Patience finally must crown. (1287-96)

The vaguely Christian connotations of the words "saints" and "patience" should not blind us to the essentially Stoic quality of the idea of victory over fortune, lot, and chance. Even if one should insist on regarding this passage as Christian, it is clear that Manoa and the Chorus finally regard Samson as an active, not a passive, hero:

> O dearly bought revenge, yet glorious!

Manoa echoes the Chorus' thought:

> *Samson* hath quit himself
> Like *Samson,* and heroicly hath finish'd
> A life Heroic, on his Enemies
> Fully reveng'd hath left them years of mourning. (1709-12)

Samson's death was of a piece with his life, and his memory will inflame the breasts of the valiant youth of Israel "To matchless valor, and adventures high" (1740).

One such valiant youth was the young Jesus of *Paradise Regained.* Although he does not mention Samson in his soliloquy in the desert, the example of an earlier deliverer springs readily to mind when he says:

> yet this not all
> To which my Spirit aspir'd; victorious deeds
> Flam'd in my heart, heroic acts; one while
> To rescue *Israel* from the *Roman* yoke,
> Then to subdue and quell o'er all the earth
> Brute violence and proud Tyrannic pow'r,
> Till truth were freed, and equity restor'd. (I.214-20)

These are precisely the terms the Chorus had used in the passage about the active hero quoted above, and Samson too had spoken of his own "great exploits" (32) and "mightiest deeds" (638) and of the promise that he "Should *Israel* from *Philistian* yoke deliver" (39). The similarities, however, only heighten the great and significant difference: the aspiration to victorious deeds is an early stage of Christ's spiritual development; it is, in fact, one of the temptations of Satan, who is the great celebrator of heroic action in *Paradise Regained*. Satan tells the devils that Christ is adorned with "amplitude of mind to greatest Deeds"; his mind, more exalted than Solomon's, is "set wholly on the accomplishment/Of greatest things." Later he tells Christ, "all thy heart is set on high designs,/High actions," and the heroes he proposes for imitation are all men of action: Alexander, Scipio Africanus, Pompey, Julius Caesar, and Judas Maccabaeus, who retired to the desert with arms; we would hardly be surprised if Satan were to add the name of Samson to this list. Satan's understanding of Christ's role as the deliverer of Israel is like Samson's understanding of his own role, and when Satan appeals to Christ's sense of zeal and duty by recounting the abominations inflicted on Israel by the Romans, he too echoes the Chorus in *Samson* when it speaks of "Tyrannic power . . . raging to pursue/The righteous and all such as honor Truth" (1275-76).

Samson's inability to rise to Christ's contempt for "ostentation vain of fleshly arm" (iii.387) is underlined by Milton in the Harapha episode. Whether or not we regard Harapha's visit as a temptation, it is clear that Samson's response is seriously flawed. Wholly admirable is his trust in the living God, his willingness to acknowledge that God has inflicted these indignities on him justly; less admirable, at best, is his eagerness to engage Harapha in single combat, his pathetic belief that by clubbing Harapha to death he will demonstrate the glory of God. The language of chivalric combat used by both Samson and Harapha places this encounter at a vast moral distance from the "great duel, not of arms" in which Christ engages the Father of all the giants of the earth. Samson, it is true, has purified his motives since the time when "swoll'n with pride" he walked about "like a petty God . . . admir'd of all and dreaded" (529-32). But while purity of heart is a necessary part of the "wisdom" that vanquishes "hellish wiles" (*PR* 1.175), it is not enough. After all, some at least of the motives that Satan proposed to Christ were beyond reproach.

A more fundamental contrast between Samson and Christ is comprehended in Michael's lines quoted earlier:

> So Law appears imperfet, and but giv'n
> With purpose to resign them in full time
> Up to a better Cov'nant, disciplin'd
> From shadowy Types to Truth, from Flesh to Spirit.

Throughout his life Milton opposed to the literalism and carnality of the Old Testament the spirituality of the New. It is the basis of his attack on the bishops, whom he calls Judaizers and whose altars and candles at noon he says were "superstitions fetched from paganism or Jewism." [2] The Jews of the Old Testament, according to Milton, were content to remain in the letter of the law and did not realize, for example, that the ceremonial vestments were merely typical foreshadowings of the inward purity of Christians.

In *Paradise Regained* it is primarily Satan who represents the fleshly, literalistic Old Testament point of view. Someone has wittily observed that the trouble with Satan is that he cannot recognize a metaphor. The most obvious example is his failure to understand the significance of the Dove. When he was at the baptism, he tells his followers, he saw Heaven unfold her crystal doors and on Christ's head "A perfect Dove descend, whate'er it meant." Christ, on the other hand, knows perfectly well what it meant:

> But as I rose out of the laving stream,
> Heaven open'd her eternal doors, from whence
> The Spirit descended on me like a Dove. (1.280-82)

In the temptations that follow, Christ's strategy with Satan is to internalize and spiritualize Satan's terms by turning them into metaphors. And Satan is so literalistic that he can't even understand a metaphor when it is explained to him. To his suggestion that Christ turn stones into bread to relieve himself and others in the wilderness with food, Christ replies, "Is it not written . . . Man lives not by Bread only, but each Word/Proceeding from the mouth of God . . . ?" And a little later he contrasts God's word to the words that proceed from Satan's oracles: "For lying is thy sustenance, thy food." But Satan returns next morning to appeal to Christ's physical hunger, telling the devils,

> And now I know he hungers where no food
> Is to be found, in the wide Wilderness.

But Christ, we know, is "fed with better thoughts" and is "hung'ring more to do [his] Father's will" (11.258-59). When he tells Satan he has no need of food, the arch-literalist is baffled. "How hast thou hunger then?" he asks (11.321), and proceeds to display his ludicrous baroque banquet. Christ counters with an oblique reference to the Eucharist:

> I can at will, doubt not, as soon as thou,
> Command a Table in this Wilderness,

[2] *The Likeliest Means to Remove Hirelings*, in Hughes, ed., *John Milton*, p. 865.

> And call swift flights of Angels ministrant
> Array'd in Glory on my cup to attend, (ii.383-86)

and ends with a contemptuous question,

> And with my hunger what hast thou to do? (ii.389)

In the temptation of the kingdoms that follows, Satan clings to his literalistic Old Testament interpretation of the role of the Messiah. Christ tells him, before the temptation is well under way, that he who reigns within himself is more a king; that to guide nations in the way of truth is yet more kingly; and that "to give a Kingdom hath been thought/Greater and nobler done, and to lay down/Far more magnanimous than to assume." But Satan hears not; he merely shifts his ground from means to motives. He appeals to Christ's sense of glory and then to his zeal and duty "to free/Thy Country from her Heathen servitude." Christ has a conception of spiritual liberty and servitude far beyond Satan's ken:

> Should I of these the liberty regard,
> Who freed, as to their ancient Patrimony,
> Unhumbl'd, unrepentant, unreform'd,
> Headlong would follow, and to thir Gods perhaps
> Of *Bethel* and of *Dan?* (iii.427-31)

But Satan persists, suggesting that Christ might ascend the throne of Tiberius and "A victor people free from servile yoke" (iv.102). "What wise and valiant man would seek to free/These thus degenerate, by themselves enslav'd," asks Christ, "Or could of inward slaves make outward free?" (iv.143-45). The baffled Satan makes one last effort of the imagination. Christ seems "otherwise inclin'd/Than to a worldly Crown," and Satan suggests to him that, as his empire must extend, "So let extend thy mind o'er all the world," ruling the Gentiles by persuasion. But this is the furthest Satan's mind will stretch, and when Christ rejects the learning of Athens, Satan admits he does not understand whether Christ's kingdom will be "Real or Allegoric." The joke is on Satan, as Northrop Frye has shown us, for Christ's kingdom, allegoric to Satan, is the only kingdom that is real.[3]

One way of defining Christ's strategy in *Paradise Regained* would be to call it a purification of the word. "In the beginning was the

---

[3] Northrop Frye, "The Typology of *Paradise Regained*," *Modern Philology*, LIII (1956), 231.

Word, and the Word was made flesh." Milton would add to this formula, "The Word was made flesh so that flesh might become word." In *Paradise Lost* when Christ incarnates himself he does not lessen or degrade his nature, but rather raises human nature to the level of divinity; when Satan incarnates himself in the serpent, he merely imbrutes his own essence.

If we turn now to *Samson Agonistes,* we will find no such metaphorical activity; at the most stones are turned into bread, but physical hunger is not transmuted into spiritual hunger. The two major motives of blindness and delivery from bondage receive only a limited metaphorical extension that falls far short of Christ's achievement in *Paradise Regained.*

Samson, for example, has insight enough to recognize that his present servitude is not so ignominious as his servitude to Dalila, and he can see that the Israelites were brought to servitude by their vices and hence prefer "Bondage with ease" to "strenuous liberty" (271), but he still thinks it possible "of inward slaves [to] make outward free" (*PR* iv.145). The insights of the Chorus are on a lower level: they regard Samson's blindness as a "Prison within Prison" (153), and they suggest that the man who can patiently endure what chance inflicts is the deliverer of himself. Manoa's apprehension is the most earthly and literalistic of all as he pathetically and ironically bustles off to arrange for Samson's ransom. In his final recognition that "death who sets all free/Hath paid his ransom now and full discharge" (1572-73) he rises no higher than the pagan conception of death as release from affliction. All these attempts to purify the ideas of bondage and deliverance remain within the limited moral and spiritual vision of paganism and Old Testament Judaism; nowhere is there a realization that because of Adam's sin man is in bondage to Satan and that Christ is his only deliverer, that it is Christ's death alone that sets all men free, and that to the faithful death is "the Gate of Life."

In the same manner the theme of blindness receives at most a moral purification. Manoa characteristically hopes for a miracle, the literal restoration of Samson's sight. The Chorus refers to Samson's "inward eyes" (1689), but they do not suggest that he can tell of things invisible to mortal sight. Samson's insight, like his insight about his bondage to Dalila, is that his present blindness is not so bad as when he "saw not how degenerately [he] serv'd" (419). When we compare Samson's limited awareness with Milton's exalted spiritualizing of blindness in the invocation to Book iii of *Paradise Lost,* are we not

justified in assuming that Samson suffers a kind of spiritual, as well
as physical, blindness?

The contrast between the old dispensation of the letter and the new
dispensation of the spirit is deliberately heightened, I suggest, by
Milton's technique of putting into the mouths of the characters words
that almost automatically call for a metaphorical interpretation by
the Christian reader. One of my students saw in the following lines an
oblique allusion to the Crucifixion:

> O dark, dark, dark, amid the blaze of noon,
> Irrecoverably dark, total Eclipse
> Without all hope of day! (80-82)

If that seems too private, more than one commentator has heard
Christian overtones in the following lines of Manoa:

> Reject not then what offer'd means, who knows
> But God hath set before us, to return thee
> Home to thy country and his sacred house, (516-18)

and

>                                 I however
> Must not omit a Father's timely care
> To prosecute the means of thy deliverance
> By ransom or how else. (601-4)

The most obvious example is the Chorus's comparison of Samson to
the Phoenix:

> So virtue giv'n for lost,
> Deprest, and overthrown, as seem'd,
> Like that self-begott'n bird
> In the *Arabian* woods embost,
> That no second knows nor third,
> And lay erewhile a Holocaust,
> From out her ashy womb now teem'd,
> Revives, reflourishes, then vigorous most
> When most unactive deem'd,
> And though her body die, her fame survives,
> A secular bird ages of lives. (1697-1707)

The comparison of Christ to the phoenix was a Christian commonplace; here, significantly, the phoenix is not even used as a symbol of
personal immortality, but only of the immortality of fame.

Alongside such terms, whose Christian significance provides an ironic counterpoint to the literal significance intended by the speakers, we find words that can only be regarded as Old Testament or pagan. The emphasis on revenge at the end of the play is the notorious example; equally pagan is the Chorus's reliance on the concepts of fortune, chance, and lot in the famous passage on patience already quoted. It is hard to avoid the conclusion that Milton, far from trying to Christianize *Samson Agonistes*, was at some pains to maintain the integrity of his Old Testament materials. Instead of collapsing Samson and Christ, he is concerned to measure the distance between various levels of awareness (represented by Manoa, the Chorus, and Samson) possible to those living under the old dispensation and the level of awareness revealed by Christ in *Paradise Regained*.

In what respect, then, is Milton's Samson like Christ? Did Milton simply turn his back on the whole tradition of Christian exegesis of the Samson story? With much of that tradition he no doubt had little sympathy. One cannot think that Milton regarded the carrying off of the gates of Azzah as a type of the harrowing of Hell; or the jawbone of the ass as a type of the Gospel; or Samson's locks as the rays of heavenly contemplation. Certainly no such fanciful resemblances found their way into *Samson Agonistes*. In the list of parallels between Samson and Christ given in Thomas Hayne's *The General View of the Holy Scriptures*, however, there is a significant item which, taken in conjunction with Arnold Stein's analysis of the meaning of Samson's *agon*, fully reveals Milton's intention. The last of Hayne's parallels reads (in part) as follows: "Christs Divinitie permitting it, he was bound, led to the Judgement hall, mocked. . . ." In the opposite column: "The spirit of God, which strengthened Sampson, permitting, he was bound, led away, mocked. . . ."[4]

Samson's agonized consciousness that he is an object of scorn and mockery is a motive that runs all through the play. As early as line 34 he complains that he has been made the "scorn and gaze" of his enemies; a little later he says he is exposed

> To daily fraud, contempt, abuse and wrong,
> Within doors, or without, still as a fool,
> In power of others, never in my own. (76-78)

[4] Thomas Hayne, *The General View of the Holy Scriptures* (London, 1640), p. 218, reproduced in F. Michael Krouse, *Milton's Samson and the Tradition* (Princeton: Princeton University Press for University of Cincinnati, 1949), facing p. 69.

When he hears the Chorus approaching he thinks it is his enemies "who come to stare/At my affliction, and perhaps to insult" (112-13), and he reverts to this topic at least twelve more times in the course of the play. The climax of this theme is reached when Samson refuses to go with the Philistine officer:

> Have they not Sword-players, and ev'ry sort
> Of Gymnic Artists, Wrestlers, Riders, Runners,
> Jugglers and Dancers, Antics, Mummers, Mimics,
> But they must pick mee out with shackles tir'd,
> And over-labor'd at thir public Mill,
> To make them sport with blind activity?
>
>                     .    .    .
>
> Can they think me so broken, so debas'd
> With corporal servitude, that my mind ever
> Will condescend to such absurd commands?
> Although thir drudge, to be thir fool or jester,
> And in my midst of sorrow and heart-grief
> To show them feats, and play before thir god,
> The worst of all indignities, yet on me
> Join'd with extreme contempt? I will not come.
>
>                                    (1323-28, 1335-42)

But he does come, and, as Stein so finely says, the man who has failed as the athlete of God succeeds as the Fool of God.[5] Is Samson himself conscious of the significance of his new role? Has he finally learned that it is humiliation that exalts? Earlier he had acknowledged that the indignities heaped on him by Harapha were inflicted justly by God; here there is no indication in the text that Samson attaches any moral or spiritual significance to his willingness to suffer public humiliation at the Philistine games. On the contrary, he obviously still thinks of himself as the athlete of God:

> If there be aught of presage in the mind,
> This day will be remarkable in my life
> By some great act, or of my days the last. (1387-89)

And it is as act, not as passion, that Manoa and the Chorus regard Samson's victory. He has revenged himself on his enemies and hero-ically has finished a life heroic. Only in a few words of the Messenger do we get a glimpse of the Samson who might have been:

---

[5] Stein, *Heroic Knowledge*, p. 196; [see above p. 63].

> He patient but undaunted where they led him,
> Came to the place . . . (1623-24)

But not to the place called Golgotha. Even in this essential parallel between Samson and Christ we are acutely aware of the difference between the "faithful champion" who destroys his enemies and the Savior who forgives and redeems his.

The harshness of the contrast between Samson's ethic and Christ's may be mitigated by regarding the destruction of the Philistines as a foreshadowing of God's terrible judgment on evil and of the Last Judgment in particular. Such an interpretation, however, robs Samson of his existential reality and makes of the play a ghostly paradigm. If, on the other hand, we view Samson first of all as a concrete individual living in a concrete historical situation, then we must insist that his significance for the Christian reader lies primarily in his inability to measure up to the heroic norm delineated in *Paradise Regained.* For it is humiliation that exalts, not the ruin of a pagan temple. Although he dimly foreshadows the humiliation of his Savior, Samson remains blind to the spiritual significance of his suffering. He cannot know, nor can Manoa and the Chorus, that they must all remain in bondage until the death of One who will in truth, not in shadow, prosecute the means of their deliverance and return them home to their Father's house.

## PART TWO

*View Points*

# *T. J. B. Spencer: Samson Agonistes* in London

Milton's *Samson Agonistes* was performed each evening for several weeks in the Church of St. Martin's-in-the-Fields in London during May 1951 by the Rock Theater Co. . . .

The directness, the austerity and the intensity of Milton's diction in this his last poetic work proved astonishingly successful as a dramatic medium. Some of the adverse criticisms we have heard about Milton's later style seemed to be irrelevant when one had listened to the powerful voice of Mr. Abraham Sofaer enunciating the lines. Milton's deliberate choice of an unembellished eloquence in this work was felt to be due not to an enfeeblement of imaginative power but to an intensification of it. To me he seemed to reveal an unexpected imaginative understanding of the necessities of dramatic diction.

Secondly, we found ourselves the spectators of a *drama*. We were not merely listening to the public recitation of a poem. In his preface Milton says, perhaps a little aggressively, that his work was not intended for the stage. But what was surprising was that the play seemed to reveal so much skilled stagecraft, although Milton's practical experience of such things can have been very slight. It shows an obvious advance on *Comus*, which *was* written for performance. It hardly emerges as an imitation of Greek tragedy. Rather, such was Milton's intensity of imagination, the devices of ancient Greek drama were effective once again. This is particularly true of the Sophoclean irony. The "dramatic irony" was, in fact, intensely dramatic and helped to unify the development of the plot. Moreover certain quiet moments in the play, which probably leave little impression on most readers, emerged as startlingly important variations in the emotional intensity of the play. Several of the characteristics of the play which have long been known to us as "literary influences" were revealed as dramatically

"Samson Agonistes *in London," by* T. J. B. Spencer. *Excerpted from a review in* Seventeenth Century News, *IX (1951), 35. Reprinted by permission of the editor,* J. Max Patrick *and Prof.* T. J. B. Spencer, *The Shakespeare Institute, University of Birmingham, England.*

effective. Thus the plausibility of Dalila was not merely an exercise in Euripidean sophistry, but a necessary revelation of Samson's history and character; the very inadequacy of his retorts to her subtle and appealing advances make the situation dramatically more convincing; his former deception by Dalila is immediately credible.

It was noticeable, too, how unobtrusive during the performance was that "personal element" which inevitably seems important to the reader. The pathos of blindness was Samson's not Milton's. The expressions of misogyny were a natural result of Samson's experience and did not necessarily reflect Milton's disappointments. The tirades against the insolence and the idolatrous rites of the Philistines seemed a convincing dramatic expression of Hebrew pride and religious fervor; the views of a disappointed Puritan on the morals of Charles II's court were hardly relevant. In brief, the impression from this performance was that the play was written with far more dramatic objectivity than is commonly supposed by readers. . . .

## E. M. W. Tillyard: Origins of *Samson Agonistes*

. . . The reason why Milton wrote an objective drama is less clear. He probably began (as after all most authors must begin) with the desire of personal expression and succeeded in becoming interested in Samson as Samson, not merely in Samson as himself. But Hanford [1] has the interesting idea that with *Samson Agonistes* Milton fulfilled his early literary program as outlined in *Reason of Church Government*. In this pamphlet Milton had mentioned 'that epic form whereof the two poems of Homer, and those other two of Virgil and Tasso, are a diffuse, and the book of Job a brief model' and had gone on to wonder 'whether those dramatic constitutions, wherein Sophocles and Euripides reign, shall be found more doctrinal and exemplary to a nation.' Hanford concludes that *Paradise Lost* is Milton's fulfilment of the 'diffuse model,' *Paradise Regained* (a good deal reminiscent of the *Book of Job*) of the 'brief model,' and *Samson Agonistes* of 'those

*Excerpted from* Milton, Part *III*, *"The Later Poems," chapter xi* "Samson Agonistes: *Its Origin*," *by E. M. W. Tillyard.* (London: Chatto & Windus Ltd., *1930; New York: Barnes & Noble, Inc., 1930), pp. 329-331. Copyright 1930 by Chatto & Windus, Ltd. Reprinted by permission of the publishers and Mrs. Veronica Sankaran.*

[1] James Holly Hanford, "*Samson Agonistes* and Milton in Old Age," reprinted above, p. 14.

dramatic constitutions, wherein Sophocles and Euripides reign'—all according to plan. This suits admirably with Hanford's larger theory, held by him too rigidly, that Milton's mind was settled and stopped growing at an early age and that his writings are a fulfilment alone, not a development. This is not the place to dispute this larger theory. I must confine myself to casting doubt on the supposed relation of *Reason of Church Government* to Milton's subsequent poems. First it must be pointed out that other projects (which Hanford ignores) are mentioned in *Reason of Church Government:* a pastoral drama on the model of the *Song of Solomon,* a tragedy on the model of *Revelation,* 'magnific odes and hymns, wherein Pindarus and Callimachus are in most things worthy.' Surely it would be more reasonable to add these to the program and argue that Milton failed to complete it, than to omit their mention altogether and argue from the more convenient items. But there is little probability of any fixed program beyond the intention of writing an epic. At one time Milton may have intended an epic, a pastoral drama, and a brief epic; at another an epic, a tragedy on the model of *Revelation,* and a series of Pindaric Odes. Once he had committed himself to writing, he would frame his program by what he had not yet succeeded in expressing. It happened that the myth of Samson and the classical form of tragedy were suited to expressing something he had yet to express after he had completed his two epics. As W. P. Ker[2] put it, '*Samson Agonistes* was not written merely as an experiment in Greek poetic form. It was written because the Greek form was the right form for something that Milton wanted to say.' I refuse to believe that, if Milton had found in the Pindaric Ode (for instance) a more suitable means of expressing what he wanted to say, he would have discarded that form for one that suited him worse, in order to carry out a supposed program of work drawn up nearly thirty years before.

## *Frank Kermode: Samson Agonistes* and Hebrew Prosody

It is well known that the rejection of Greek lyric poetry in *Paradise Regain'd* (IV.331 ff.) is not without precedent either in Milton's own

---

"Samson Agonistes *and Hebrew Poetry," by Frank Kermode. Excerpted from an article similarly titled in the* Durham University Journal, *XIV (1953), 59-63. Copyright © 1953 by the University of Durham. Reprinted by permission of the publisher.*

[2] *The Art of Poetry* (Oxford: The Clarendon Press, 1925).

works[1] or in earlier literature.[2] There is, however, one aspect of the rejection which seems not to be generally understood; and here we find a clue to the verse of the chorus in *Samson Agonistes*.

It will be remembered that Christ finds

> All our Law and Story strew'd
> With Hymns, our Psalms with artful terms inscrib'd (IV.334-5);

he describes the Greek poetry as derivative from the Hebrew, and

> unworthy to compare
> With *Sion's* songs, to all true tasts excelling,
> Where God is prais'd aright, and Godlike men (IV.346-8).

Milton refers to the passages in the Old Testament which were commonly, though not universally, supposed to have been written in verse, like Job, the Psalms, certain portions of Genesis, Deuteronomy, Isaiah and Jeremiah. The main interest was in Job and the Psalms, which latter were, as Sidney said, "Fully written in meeter as all learned Hebricians agree, although the rules be not fully found." [3] This opinion was often repeated and occasionally contested. But on one point all were agreed, that the Psalms were exceptionally rich in the figures of poetic. It was sometimes suggested that the Psalter contained all the figures and tropes, but in any case it was not disputed that it was in this, as in all other respects, superior to pagan poetry, and specifically to Pindar's, with which it was most often compared. It is clear that Milton's "with artful terms inscrib'd" refers to this belief, though Newton's assertion that the allusion is to "the inscriptions prefixed to the beginning of the several psalms" (a rather unimaginative guess) is repeated as late as the edition of E. H. Blakeney (1932). Christ is asserting the supremacy of the Hebrew songs "not in their divine argument alone, but in the very critical art of composition." [4]

Scholars who believed that these highly figurative compositions had been written in verse labored to discover the lost secret. We are much

[1] John Milton, *The Reason of Church Government; Works*, ed. F. A. Patterson, New York: Columbia University Press, 1931), iii, 238.

[2] From the many authors who make this point one may choose two whose work seems to have interested Milton: Giles Fletcher, in his Preface to *Christ's Victory and Triumph* (1610), and Cowley in the Preface to the 1656 Quarto of his poems.

[3] Philip Sidney, *Defense of Poetry*; Gregory Smith, ed., *Elizabethan Critical Essays* (Oxford: The Clarendon Press, 1904), i, 155.

[4] Milton, *Reason of Church Government*.

indebted to Mr. Israel Baroway for elucidating their enquiries; and this paragraph does him the injustice of briefly abstracting his papers[5] for my purposes. The classical tradition, based on St. Jerome, held that the verse of Job and the Psalms was quantitative, and analogous to the verse of Pindar. This view had its most elaborate expression in the *Davidis Lyra* of Franciscus Gomarus (1637), but by that time support for it had diminished, and the work of Gomarus is in fact an unintentional reduction to absurdity of the Hieronymic principle; he solves every anomaly with a new law until his system becomes fantastically complex. J. J. Scaliger and the elder Vossius rejected the position, denied that the Psalms were written in verse, and, though working in a rival tradition stemming from St. Augustine, availed themselves of a hint in Jerome's Preface to Job that the book was occasionally accentual rather than quantitative; they suggested a parallel with the accentual *Politici* of late Greek poetry.[6] Mr. Baroway credits Scaliger with the first glimpse of the modern theory of the *parallelismus membrorum* in Hebrew poetry, and of "the generally accepted theory of a free accentual rhythm which considers only the syllables receiving the main accent, and disregards the intervening ones." [7]

There remains another theory which is also accentual, but which does not exclude the Psalms; Mr. Baroway conjectures that it passed from Ibn Chabib to Tremellius and possibly to Steuchus; and from the first, or from both of these, to Sidney. This view encouraged the belief that vernacular accentual measures were closer to the original Hebrew than the quantitative verse of the classical languages. [George] Wither elaborately defends this position in his *Preparation to the Psalter.*[8]

Wither's work (which in other ways invites the attention of historians of criticism) exalts the Psalms above all other poetry, in the first place because of their divine inspiration. This is conveyed to the translator.

[5] *Journal of English and Germanic Philology*, xxxii (1933), 447-80; *English Literary History*, ii (1935), 66-91; *ELH.* viii (1941), 119-42; *ELH.* xvii (1950), 115-35.

[6] The πολιτικοί [*politici*] described by J. C. Scaliger, *Poetics Libri Septem*, II xxix (3rd Edition, 1586) 180. "In late Byzantine literature there is a large class of miscellaneous poetry in the popular fifteen-syllable 'political' meter, at first unrhymed, then rhymed." F. H. Marshall, in *Byzantium*, ed. N. H. Baynes and A. St. L. B. Moss (Oxford: Oxford University Press, 1948), p. 249. See also J. M. Hussey, *Church and Learning in the Byzantine Empire* (Oxford: Oxford University Press, 1937), pp. 32-3.

[7] *ELH.* xvii, 133.

[8] Publication of the Spenser Society, No. 37 (London, 1884).

ʹ                                     The Deitie that guides my quill
                            Haunts not *Parnassus,* but fair *Sion* Hill.[9]

David was a poet; and this, as Sidney had said, confutes the vulgar
attack against all poetry. The Psalms exhibit all the tropes and figures
in unique concentration. Hebrew verse is not quantitative but accentual; quantity is foreign to the Hebrew tongue. As the Jews themselves allege, "their *Poems* consist of divers *Numbers* intermixt, sometimes equally, sometimes unequally, and oftentimes with *Rymes* in
the periods of Sentences; not much unlike some of our *English Numbers* . . ." There is more irregularity than modern English usage
permits, but "though the *Verse,* in the Syllables may sometimes seem
too long or too short, and the Rymes appear to the eye in writing,
not so perfect as ours are: yet they [the judicious] will conceive that
there may bee somewhat to bee observed in the pronuntiation, which
will both make the number of Syllables equall, and the *Ryme* full." [10]
Wither cites, as a characteristically imperfect Davidic rhyme, *dreshe—
gnesheb.* Thus the way to the secrets of Hebrew prosody is not through
Greek, but English verse; and without forgetting that in his customary
irregularity of rhythm, rhyme and length of stave the ancient poet
has made it very difficult for us, we may claim to know at least how
best to convey his work in the vernacular.

Wither is original neither in his rejection of quantity nor in his
views on Hebrew rhyme, which Puttenham had expressed quite
casually many years earlier.[11] But his work gives us some notion of
the opinions current early in the century, and it is fair to assume that
Milton was familiar with the whole problem; doubtless he had his own
ideas about it. At any rate he would be perfectly acquainted with the
idea that there were unusual possibilities in the English language for
the imitation of Hebrew lyric metres. (He probably had it in mind
when he made his little-studied versions of the Psalms.[12]) In *Paradise*

    [9] p. 139. Cf. Falkland's commendatory verses to Sandys upon his version of the
psalms: Sandys has "chang'd Parnassus mount to Sion's Hill." (Sandys, *Poetical
Works, ed. Hooper* [London, 1872] i. 86.) The passage has something in common
with *P.R.,* iv, 332 ff.
    [10] pp. 59-61.
    [11] [George Puttenham] *Arte of English Poesie,* ed. Willcock and Walker (Cam-
bridge: The University Press, 1936), p. 10. "But the Hebrues & Chaldees who were
more ancient than the Greekes, did not only use a metricall Poesie, but also with
the same maner of rime, as hath bene of late observed by learned men".
    [12] Recently W. B. Hunter, Jr., suggested [*Philological Quarterly,* xxviii (1949),
125-44] that Milton's later prosody was in fact based on a study of the English
metrical psalters.

*Regain'd* he expressed an unequivocal opinion that the praise of Godlike men was the matter of the songs of Sion, not of Parnassus. The tragedy which appeared with *Paradise Regain'd* is certainly concerned with "The Holiest of Holies and his Saints:" does it bear no trace of the song which excelled to all true tastes?

*Samson Agonistes* is of course Greek in structure, and Milton in his Epistle takes pains to harmonize this with the divine nature of his theme. But he disclaims any design to reproduce the characteristic structure of the Greek chorus, labelling his choruses "*Monostrophic* or rather *Apolelymenon* . . . being divided into stanzas and pauses they may be called *Allaeostropha.*" All these unfamiliar expressions are explained in J. C. Scaliger's *Poetices Libri,*[13] and they all refer to the strophe itself—to the absence of formal patterns in the strophe, not to the metrical irregularities of the several lines. The terms could be quite correctly applied to the Pindaric of Cowley. Milton, then, tells us nothing whatsoever about the system of his choral verse except that it is not divided as the Greek tragedians divided theirs.

It has, I think, been generally assumed that he was imitating Greek measures in the choruses.[14] Bridges thought this the only possible explanation, but it has never been satisfactorily worked out; as Bridges himself says, "The opinions which critics have ventured on the versification of the choruses in *Samson Agonistes* would be sufficient proof that they had met with something not well understood, even if they had never misinterpreted the rhythm." [15] Attempts to scan the choruses according to the book result in confusion strangely like that of Gomarus; and the rhyming, however intermittent, is a stumbling-block. But Milton himself provides a clue when he says he has abandoned the strophic chorus; these are not imitations of the Greek, though it may, he suggests, be worth mentioning that the Greeks would have called this kind of chorus *Apolelymenon,* etc. Instead of imitation Greek choruses he writes passages made up of lines various and irregular in length, exceedingly free in accent, and occasionally rhyming. And this was the practice also of the Psalmist and the author of Job, as some critics read them. Job, in particular, was obviously much in Milton's mind in his later years.

It is not a far step from *Paradise Regain'd* to the rejection of the

---

[13] II, xxv, pp. 173-4.

[14] G. L. Finney (*Publications of the Modern Language Association of America,* lviii [1943] 649-664) suggested a closer contact with Italian melodrama.

[15] Robert Bridges, *Milton's Prosody* (London: Oxford University Press, 1901), p. 30.

Greek choral ode; Milton must have had Sophocles and especially Pindar in mind when he wrote the passage in *Paradise Regain'd.* (He may also have been thinking of Pindar's modern imitators.) It is not unreasonable to suppose that when, in his later poem, he had to write for a chorus he decided to provide it with non-Parnassian imitations of *"Sion's* songs, to all true tasts excelling." . . .*

### *Arnold Stein:* Manoa

Manoa introduces the most human voice into the drama, the one with the widest range, and a full dramatic and natural privilege to express that range. The voice is both public, saying what ordinary men might feel, and individual to his character and to his position as father. Finally, as spokesman for ordinary humanity and as participant in the drama, he will be privileged to express a purified human response to the tragic experience.

The first effect is different and shocking, partly because of the quality of the new voice, which is recklessly willing to articulate attitudes not yet articulated; but partly also because that new voice repeats what has already been said, but turns it peremptorily into the special expression of a new and forceful dramatic position. The Chorus, in its first recognition of Samson, spoke with awe and pity (and with some remarkable poetic rhythms):

> This, this is he; softly a while,
> Let us not break in upon him;
> O change beyond report, thought, or belief.

Manoa roughly and abruptly condenses: "O miserable change! is this the man . . ." He continues, as the Chorus did, to mark the difference by recalling what Samson was, and in a similar rhythm: "That invincible *Samson.*" But he does not celebrate Samson's previous glory so much as use it for a rhetorical contrast which is unsparing. The Chorus drew its moral, that of medieval tragedy but, I think, not Milton's: "O mirror of our fickle state." Manoa draws a similar kind

---

*"Manoa." Excerpted from "A Little Onward" in* Heroic Knowledge: An Interpretation of *Paradise Regained* and *Samson Agonistes, by Arnold Stein. (Minneapolis: University of Minnesota Press, 1957), pp. 148-50. Copyright © 1957 by the University of Minnesota. Reprinted by permission of the publisher.*

* An examination of the imperfect rhymes in *Samson Agonistes* follows—ED.

of moral, as platitudinous, perhaps as misplaced, but certainly over-
personalized:

> O ever failing trust
> In mortal strength! and oh what not in man
> Deceivable and vain! Nay what thing good
> Pray'd for, but often proves our woe, our bane?
> I pray'd for Children.

The Chorus, whatever its ambivalence toward Samson, did not see
him as ridiculous, though its presence reminded Samson of the fact.
But Manoa insists relentlessly on the external view that mirrors what
we know to be an internal torment:

> The miracle of men: then in an hour
> Select, and Sacred, Glorious for a while,
> Ensnar'd, assaulted, overcome, led bound,
> Thy Foes derision, Captive, Poor, and Blind
> Into a Dungeon thrust, to work with Slaves.

Those are hard words. They sing and proverb the great folly, and
answer by specific demonstration the question the Chorus left politely
unanswered. Manoa says nothing that the hero does not know, but
(is it irrelevant to surmise?) Samson may need somebody to say this.
Perhaps it is not too farfetched to think the same of Manoa's calling
God's justice into question. So far we have had only one side of that
matter, and this is a drama. Manoa's point of view is frankly personal:
these were his prayers, his gifts, granted with pomp and solemnity,
"desirable, to tempt." The loss, and even the ridicule, somehow seem
chiefly his. And when he moves from the obviously personal complaint
to the larger questioning of God's judgment, it still is plainly the
special pleading, or complaint, of a passionate participant in a particular case.

It is easy to misjudge Manoa, especially if one is unacquainted with
the Haggadah, or has never heard, on a grandfather's knee, the Old
Testament God spoken of with respectful but authoritative familiarity.
Manoa represents a people with an old, direct, and, as it were, fam-
ily relationship to God; with no real history, even in error, not
responding to or against that relationship. The certainty of the relationship makes possible unofficial latitude unthinkable or blas-
phemous in religions of more recent establishment. Milton's Manoa is
complaining against God, and he can hardly be unaware, any more
than Samson and the Chorus, of what he is doing. "For this did the

Angel twice descend?" But lamentations are not inconsistent with true patience or true piety. He is transgressing and, I conjecture, he knows that God knows it, and that this is the grief of the father Manoa speaking, and not the piety of the son Manoa. Let me illustrate this from a brilliant fiction. In Mann's *Young Joseph,* Jacob, grieving for his lost boy, has gone too far in expostulating with God. Eliezer calls him to task and Jacob replies:

> Ah, thou God's-defender . . . Thou hypocrite . . . For what thou sayest I too could say, and thou knowest I am not duller of sense than thou. But I speak to Him otherwise, and even so am nearer to Him than thou! For one must defend God against His defenders, and protect Him against those who would protect Him. Thinkest thou He is a man, even of overwhelming power, and it is His side thou must espouse against me, a worm? When thou callest Him eternally great, thou utterest merely wind, if thou knowest not that God is still above God, still everlastingly above Himself, and will punish from above, where He is my healing and my reliance and where thou art not, if thou regardest thyself as between Him and me![1]

Manoa, to Milton's credit, is complex, and I cannot present the whole case for my conjecture now. . . .

## John M. Steadman: Milton's Harapha and Goliath

The primary source of Milton's giant is . . . Biblical rather than secular. Though classical tragedy and Renaissance comedy may have been contributing influences, his character and significance derive largely from I Samuel 17, and his name from II Samuel 21. Milton introduced him into the story of Samson on the analogy of Goliath in the story of David, in order to convey the same moral opposition which had been manifested in David's duel—the antithesis between the Hebrew's trust in God and disdain of fleshly weapons and the Philistine's pride and carnal reliance. Both Goliath and Harapha trust in "glorious arms" for "safety," but this is a false security, a

*"Milton's Harapha and Goliath," by John M. Steadman. Excerpted from an article similarly titled in the* Journal of English and Germanic Philology, LX *(October, 1961), 795. Copyright © 1961 by the University of Illinois Press. Reprinted by the permission of the publisher.*

[1] Tr. Lowe-Porter (New York: Knopf, 1935), p. 292 ff.

*vana salus.*[1] "The Lord saveth not with sword and spear," and both giants, for all their strength are ignominiously defeated by their un-armed opponents. The true prototype of the spiritual duel between Samson and Harapha is the *monomachia* between David and Goliath. In the encounter between a physically handicapped "hero of faith" and a Philistine giant in full armor, Milton found an ideal vehicle for the ethical opposition between *fiducia in Deo* and *fiducia carnalis.*

## *Northrop Frye:* Notes on the Tragic Hero

The tragic hero is typically on top of the wheel of fortune, halfway between human society on the ground and the something greater in the sky. Prometheus, Adam, and Christ hang between heaven and earth, between a world of paradisal freedom and a world of bondage. Tragic heroes are so much the highest points in their human landscape that they seem the inevitable conductors of the power about them, great trees more likely to be struck by lightning than a clump of grass. Conductors may of course be instruments as well as victims of the divine lightning: Milton's Samson destroys the Philistine temple with himself, and Hamlet nearly exterminates the Danish court in his own fall. . . .

Christianity, . . . sees tragedy as an episode in the divine comedy, the larger scheme of redemption and resurrection. The sense of tragedy as a prelude to comedy seems almost inseparable from anything ex-plicitly Christian. The serenity of the final double chorus in the St. Matthew Passion would hardly be attainable if composer and audience

---

*"Notes of the Tragic Hero," by Northrop Frye. Excerpted from the chapter "The Mythos of Autumn: Tragedy" in* Anatomy of Criticism *(Princeton: Princeton University Press, 1957), pp. 207, 215, 220-21. Copyright © 1957 by Princeton University Press. Reprinted by permission of the publisher.*

[1] Cf. Rabanus' comment on the Israelites' battles with four Philistine giants in II Sam. 21 (*Patrologia Latina,* CIX, col. 114): "Quid autem quatuor bella ista David et servorum ejus contra Palaestinos significant, nisi bellum Christi, quod omni tem-porae istius vitae in membris suis contra perfidos quosque istius saeculi, et contra spiritales nequitias incessanter agit? . . . Unde Psalmista ex persona Ecclesiae confi-denter dicit: 'Vana salus hominis. In Deo faciemus virtutem, et ipse ad nihilum de-ducet tribulantes nos (*Psal.* LIX).' " [. . . "what do those four battles moreover of David and his servants against the Philistines signify, if not the struggle of Christ, which at all times in this life he wages in his body against spiritual vileness and against every faithless one of this age? . . . Whence the Psalmist in the person of the church confidently says: 'Vain is the help of man. Through God we shall do valiantly: for he it is that shall tread down our enemies.' "—ED.]

did not know that there was more to the story. Nor would the death
of Samson lead to "calm of mind, all passion spent," if Samson were
not a prototype of the rising Christ, associated at the appropriate moment with the phoenix. . . .

. . . corresponding to the central quest-theme of romance, is tragedy
in which a strong emphasis is thrown on the success or completeness of
the hero's achievement. The Passion belongs here, as do all tragedies
in which the hero is in any way related to or a prototype of Christ,
like *Samson Agonistes*. The paradox of victory within tragedy may be
expressed by a double perspective in the action. Samson is a buffoon
of a Philistine carnival and simultaneously a tragic hero to the Israelites, but the tragedy ends in triumph and the carnival in catastrophe. . . .

At the end of [the sixth phase of tragedy, "a world of shock and
horror"], we reach a point of demonic epiphany where we see or
glimpse the undisplaced demonic vision, the vision of the *Inferno*. Its
chief symbols, besides the prison and the madhouse, are the instruments of a torturing death, the cross under the sunset being the
antithesis of the tower under the moon. A strong element of demonic
ritual in public punishments and similar mob amusements is ex-
ploited by tragic and ironic myth. Breaking on the wheel becomes
Lear's wheel of fire; bear-baiting is an image for Gloucester and Macbeth, and for the crucified Prometheus the humiliation of exposure,
the horror of being watched, is a greater misery than the pain. *Derkou
theama* (behold the spectacle; get your staring over with) is his
bitterest cry. The inability of Milton's blind Samson to stare back is
his greatest torment, and one which forces him to scream at Delila, in
one of the most terrible passages of all tragic drama, that he will tear
her to pieces if she touches him.

## W. H. Auden: Christianity and Art

Art is compatible with polytheism and with Christianity, but not
with philosophical materialism; science is compatible with philosophical materialism and with Christianity, but not with polytheism. No

artist or scientist, however, can feel comfortable as a Christian; every artist who happens also to be a Christian wishes he could be a polytheist; every scientist in the same position that he could be a philosophical materialist. And with good reason. In a polytheist society, the artists are its theologians; in a materialist society, its theologians are the scientists. To a Christian, unfortunately, both art and science are secular activities, that is to say, small beer.

No artist, qua artist, can understand what is meant by *God is Love* or *Thou shalt love thy neighbor* because he doesn't care whether God and men are loving or unloving; no scientist, qua scientist, can understand what is meant because he doesn't care whether to-be-loving is a matter of choice or a matter of compulsion.

To the imagination, the sacred is self-evident. It is as meaningless to ask whether one believes or disbelieves in Aphrodite or Ares as to ask whether one believes in a character in a novel; one can only say that one finds them true or untrue to life. To believe in Aphrodite and Ares merely means that one believes that the poetic myths about them do justice to the forces of sex and aggression as human beings experience them in nature and their own lives. That is why it is possible for an archaeologist who digs up a statuette of a god or goddess to say with fair certainty what kind of divinity it represents.

Similarly, to the imagination, the godlike or heroic man is self-evident. He does extraordinary deeds that the ordinary man cannot do, or extraordinary things happen to him.

The Incarnation, the coming of Christ in the form of a servant who cannot be recognized by the eye of flesh and blood, but only by the eye of faith, puts an end to all claims of the imagination to be the faculty which decides what is truly sacred and what is profane. A pagan god can appear on earth in disguise but, so long as he wears his disguise, no man is expected to recognize him nor can. But Christ appears looking just like any other man, yet claims that He is the Way, the Truth and the Life, and that no man can come to God the Father except through Him. The contradiction between the profane appearance and the sacred assertion is impassible to the imagination.

It is impossible to represent Christ on the stage. If he is made dramatically interesting, he ceases to be Christ and turns into a Hercules or a Svengali. Nor is it really possible to represent him in the visual arts for, if he were visually recognizable, he would be a god of the pagan kind. The best the painter can do is to paint either the Bambino with the Madonna or the dead Christ on the cross, for every baby and every corpse seems to be both individual and universal, *the* baby, *the* corpse. But neither a baby nor a corpse can say *I am the Way, etc.*

To a Christian, the godlike man is not the hero who does extraordinary deeds, but the holy man, the saint, who does good deeds. But the gospel defines a good deed as one done in secret, hidden, so far as it is possible, even from the doer, and forbids private prayer and fasting in public. This means that art, which by its nature can only deal with what can and should be manifested, cannot portray a saint.

There can no more be a "Christian" art than there can be a Christian science or a Christian diet. There can only be a Christian spirit in which an artist, a scientist, works or does not work. A painting of the Crucifixion is not necessarily more Christian in spirit than a still life, and may very well be less.

I sometimes wonder if there is not something a bit questionable, from a Christian point of view, about all works of art which make overt Christian references. They seem to assert that there is such a thing as a Christian culture, which there cannot be. Culture is one of Caesar's things. One cannot help noticing that the great period of "religious" painting coincided with the period when the Church was a great temporal power.

The only kind of literature which has gospel authority is the parable, and parables are secular stories with no overt religious reference. . . .

## A. S. P. Woodhouse: The Possibility of Christian Tragedy

. . . The question has often been asked whether a Christian tragedy is really possible. No doubt on a total view Christianity presents the drama of existence as a divine comedy—or at most a divine tragicomedy—in which the overruling power is the Supreme Goodness and whatever or whoever opposes it is finally eliminated. Whether their fate is in any negotiable sense tragic is a question that need not detain us: it no more arises than does the question whether in *Samson*

*"The Possibility of Christian Tragedy," by A. S. P. Woodhouse. Excerpted from "Tragic Effect in* Samson Agonistes," *University of Toronto Quarterly, XXVIII (1958-59), pp. 219-222. Copyright © 1958 by the University of Toronto Press. Reprinted by permission of the publisher.*

*Agonistes* the fate of the Philistines is tragic. If such a subject were ever given tragic treatment, it would have to be in a pagan, not a Christian context. If a Christian tragedy is possible, then its subject will be the saved, or those on the way to being saved, not the utterly lost. And clearly in the ample confines of the divine comedy there is plenty of room for tragic episodes. "I now must change/Those notes to tragic," writes Milton, as he introduces the subject of the first sin, and the first repentance, and their consequences. Christianity never denies the power of sin and suffering, though it envisages a final escape from them. In suffering, indeed, it discovers a new dimension. "Prosperity," said Bacon, "is the blessing of the Old Testament; adversity is the blessing of the New." This idea has entered deeply into the Christian consciousness, and not with the theologically minded alone: it receives its recognition not only in *Samson Agonistes,* but also, for example, in *Lear,* and even Cleopatra can say, "My desolation does begin to make/A better life." This is not theology: it is a profoundly true apprehension of one of the possibilities of human experience, on which Christianity has seized, and it is pregnant with drama, as Shakespeare knows and so does Milton.

Suffering may be the lot of either sinner or martyr, and Samson is both. He has sinned, and through suffering he has progressed to self-knowledge and repentance, the necessary prelude to readmission to God's service. But now God's service is martyrdom, if not precisely the usual kind. Patience, as the Chorus observes,

> is most oft the exercise
> Of saints, the trial of their fortitude,
> Making them each his own deliverer,
> And victor over all
> That tyranny or fortune can inflict. (1287-91)

This, however, is not the way of tragedy, and Samson is called upon to play a more active rôle: to be his own deliverer in a more literal sense and to achieve therewith a victory that dwarfs all his former triumphs. But suffering, though it may be a means of grace, is suffering still, and death, though it be the price of such a victory, and though it even come as a release from suffering, is still death. Thus some of the ingredients of tragedy are certainly available; and it only remains to be asked what the poet has been able to do with them. What Milton has done in respect of the action we have seen: he has made the way of repentance and restoration, the way back to God, also the way that leads inevitably to the catastrophe, and has thus achieved at a stroke the only kind of irony that is at once compatible with a Christian outlook and as potent as any to be found in tragedy anywhere. Moreover, he has shown the necessity which thus conjoins Samson's salvation and victory with his death to be no arbitrary imposition of the overruling Power, but the outcome of Samson's conduct—of his sin and of his subsequent repentance. That his repentance is achieved under the impulsion of divine grace does not alter the fact that it is Samson's own. If God is present and operative in the tragedy (as he must be in a Christian view) at least he does not operate arbitrarily—or from a machine!

So much for the poem, if it stopped short with the catastrophe. It does not. The conclusion, as we have also seen, is directed wholly to reconciliation, to mitigating the sense of disaster: first on the human level, and, when that is completed, by invoking the overruling Power, by showing the place of Samson's sacrifice, of his whole experience, in the providential order of God, who does not force men's wills but nevertheless controls the event. The emphasis of this comment is justified not only on doctrinal but on artistic grounds. The very strength of the element of tragic irony in the action both permits and demands it. And the irony and the resolution of irony alike depend on the fact that this is a Christian tragedy: that is to say, a tragedy which, however scrupulously it adheres to classical conventions, is written unfalteringly from a Christian point of view. . . .

In that possibility [of a Christian tragedy] Milton, clearly, believed; but his artist's intuition taught him that it could be realized only under certain conditions. The first was the provision of a strong element of tragic irony in the pattern of the action. The second was a resolution of that irony by a final appeal to God's providential order, to the rhythm as it were of the divine comedy. Nor was this all. If one was to achieve an effect truly tragic, one must focus attention on the hero, and must so present his response to the outward pressures of circumstance, and the inward impulsions of grace, as to render that response intelligible in purely human terms. And here Milton's former sense of a dichotomy in Samson's motivation came to his aid; only now it presented itself not as a pair of alternatives but as two forces working to a common end: "celestial vigour" *and* "plain heroic magnitude of mind." The sense of Samson as heroic individual does not stop short with the catastrophe: it extends to the comment. The reconciliation, the mitigating of the sense of disaster, is worked out in purely human terms before the larger rhythm of the divine comedy is invoked, lest that rhythm should not only resolve the tragic irony of the action, but dissolve the whole tragic effect.

# Chronology of Important Dates

| Milton | Public Events |
|---|---|
| | |

<table>
<tr><td>1608</td><td>December 9, John Milton born in Bread Street, Cheapside, London.</td></tr>
<tr><td>1620</td><td>Admission to St. Paul's School.</td></tr>
<tr><td>1629</td><td>Receives A.B. degree, Christ's College, Cambridge; composes On the Morning of Christ's Nativity.</td></tr>
<tr><td>1632-38</td><td>Resides at Horton, Buckinghamshire.</td></tr>
<tr><td>1634</td><td>A Mask (Comus) performed at Ludlow Castle, September 29.</td></tr>
<tr><td>1637</td><td>Writes Lycidas.</td></tr>
<tr><td>1638-39</td><td>Travels abroad, chiefly in Italy.</td></tr>
</table>

**Milton**

1608   December 9, John Milton born in Bread Street, Cheapside, London.

1620   Admission to St. Paul's School.

1629   Receives A.B. degree, Christ's College, Cambridge; composes *On the Morning of Christ's Nativity*.

1632-38   Resides at Horton, Buckinghamshire.

1634   *A Mask (Comus)* performed at Ludlow Castle, September 29.

1637   Writes *Lycidas*.

1638-39   Travels abroad, chiefly in Italy.

1639

1640

**Public Events**

1639   War with Scotland (First Bishops' War).

1640   Second Bishops' War. Long Parliament. Impeachment of Stafford and Laud. Ship-money and canons declared illegal.

1641-60   Writes series of prose tracts, including pamphlets against prelacy (1641-42); divorce tracts (1643-45); *Of Education, Areopagitica* (1644); *The Tenure of Kings and Magistrates, Eikonoklastes* (1649); *Defensio pro Populo Anglicano* (1651); *Defensio Secunda* (1654); *Defensio pro se* (1655); and *The Ready and Easy Way to Establish a Free Commonwealth* (1660).

| | Milton | Public Events |
|---|---|---|
| 1642 | Weds Mary Powell, separation following within six weeks; reconciliation in late summer, 1645. | Outbreak of Civil War. |
| 1643 | | Ordinance for licensing the press. |
| 1644 | | First major Parliamentary victory at Marston Moor. |
| 1645 | Publishes minor poems. | Prayer Book abolished; Laud executed. |
| 1645-46 | Working on *De Doctrina Christiana.* | |
| 1646 | | King Charles flees to Scots; surrender of Royalist headquarters at Oxford. |
| 1648 | | Second Civil War. |
| 1649 | Receives appointment as Secretary for Foreign Tongues to Council of State. | January 30: Execution of Charles I. |
| 1651-52 | Total blindness commences. | |
| 1652 | Death of Mary Powell. | |
| 1653 | | Establishment of Protectorate. |
| 1656 | Marries Katherine Woodcock (d. 1658). | |
| 1658 | | September 3: Death of Oliver Cromwell. |
| 1660 | | The Restoration: Charles II enters London (May 29). |
| 1663 | Marries Elizabeth Minshull (d. 1727). | |
| 1667 | First publication of *Paradise Lost* (2nd ed., 1674). | |
| 1671 | First publication of *Paradise Regained* and *Samson Agonistes* | |
| 1674 | Dies November 8. | |

# Notes on the Editor and Contributors

GALBRAITH M. CRUMP is Professor of English at Kenyon College, and the editor of *The Poems and Translations of Thomas Stanley* (1962), and *Poems on Affairs of State,* Vol. IV (1968).

DON CAMERON ALLEN is Sir William Osler Professor of English at Johns Hopkins University, and the author of *The Legend of Noah* (1949), *The Harmonious Vision* (1954), and *Doubt's Boundless Sea* (1964).

W. H. AUDEN is the celebrated poet, playwright, and critic. He is the author of *The Dyer's Hand and Other Essays* (1948), *The Shield of Achilles* (1955), and *Homage to Clio* (1960).

ARTHUR E. BARKER is Professor of English at the University of Illinois, and the author of *Milton and the Puritan Dilemma* (1942).

NORTHROP FRYE is Principal, Victoria College, University of Toronto, and the author of *The Anatomy of Criticism* (1957), and *The Return to Eden* (1965).

JAMES HOLLY HANFORD is Professor emeritus of Western Reserve University, and the author of *John Milton, Englishman* (1949), and *A Milton Handbook* (4th ed., 1946).

FRANK KERMODE is Professor of English, University College, London, and the editor of *The Tempest* (Arden Shakespeare, 1954). He is also the author of *The Romantic Image* (1957) and *The Sense of an Ending* (1967).

F. MICHAEL KROUSE was a former Professor of English at the University of Cincinnati, and the author of *Milton's Samson and the Christian Tradition* (1949).

WILLIAM G. MADSEN is Professor of English at Emory University, and the author of "The Idea of Nature in Milton's Poetry," in *Three Studies in the Renaissance: Sidney, Jonson, and Milton* (1958).

WILLIAM R. PARKER is Distinguished Service Professor of English at Indiana University, and the author of *Milton's Debt to Greek Tragedy in Samson Agonistes* (1937), and *Milton's Contemporary Reputation* (1940).

T. J. B. SPENCER is Professor of English at Birmingham University and the Director of the Shakespeare Institute. He is also the author of *The*

*Tyranny of Shakespeare* (1959), and *Byron and the Greek Tradition* (1960).

JOHN M. STEADMAN is a Member of the Research Staff in English Literature at the Henry E. Huntington Library.

ARNOLD STEIN is Professor of English at the University of Washington, and the author of *Answerable Style* (1953), *Heroic Knowledge* (1957), and *John Donne's Lyrics: The Eloquence of Action* (1962).

E. M. W. TILLYARD was a former Master of Jesus College, Cambridge. Author of *Milton* (1930), *The Miltonic Setting* (1938), and *The Elizabethan World Picture* (1943).

A. S. P. WOODHOUSE was a former Professor of English at University College, Toronto, and the author of *Puritanism and Liberty* (1938).

# Selected Bibliography

## Editions

The standard edition of the poetry is *The Works of John Milton,* ed. Frank Allen Patterson. New York: Columbia University Press, 1931-38 (*S.A.,* Vol. 1, Pt. a). Thoroughly annotated editions are *Paradise Regained, The Minor Poems,* and *Samson Agonistes,* ed. Merritt Y. Hughes, New York: Odyssey Press, 1937; *Samson Agonistes,* ed. F. T. Prince, London: Oxford University Press, 1957; and *Milton's Dramatic Poems,* ed. Geoffrey and Margaret Bullough, University of London: The Athlone Press, 1958.

## Secondary Sources

In addition to the works represented by the articles in this volume, the following titles are valuable to a study of *Samson Agonistes:* Sir R. C. Jebb, *Samson Agonistes and the Hellenic Drama,* London: H. Frowde (1908), provides the primary statement in the Hellenic-Hebraic debate over the play's dramatic tone and spirit; Sir H. J. C. Grierson, *Milton and Wordsworth: Poets and Prophets: A Study of their Reactions to Political Events,* Cambridge: Cambridge University Press, 1937, Chap. VI, after elaborate investigation of relation between Milton's life and art, Grierson briefly considers *Samson Agonistes,* finding that "in no poem since *Lycidas* have the poet and critic of life been so at one"; Gretchen L. Finney, "Chorus in *Samson Agonistes,*" *Publications of the Modern Language Association,* LVIII (1943), pp. 649-64, offers a specialized study of the chorus in relation to its possible models in the seventeenth-century Italian musical drama; Una Ellis-Fermor, "*Samson Agonistes* and Religious Drama," *The Frontiers of Drama,* London: Methuen, 1945, pp. 17-33, perceptively considers the limitations of religious experience in relation to dramatic form, while evaluating the success of Milton's play in pushing back the boundaries of drama; Ernest S. Sprott, "The Prosody of *Samson Agonistes,*" *Milton's Art of Prosody,* Oxford: Basil Blackwell, 1953, pp. 129-33, gives a succinct, Bridgean statement of the complexities and perplexities of these special effects; John M. Steadman, " 'Faithful Champion':

The Theological Basis of Milton's Hero of Faith," *Anglia*, LXXVII (1959), pp. 12-28, convincingly conceives the play in terms of Samson's spiritual rebirth through repentance and faith, virtues which add to the Old Testament figure's heroism, since he lived before the Promise; William Empson, "Delilah," *Milton's God*, London: Chatto and Windus, 1961, pp. 211-28, makes an entertaining *advocatus Dalilae;* Watson Kirckonnell, *That Invincible Samson: The Theme of* Samson Agonistes *in World Literature with Translations of the Major Analogues*, Toronto: University of Toronto Press, 1964, translates five early versions of the Samson story from Dutch, Italian, and Latin literature and provides a descriptive catalogue of other major analogues; Paul R. Sellin, "Milton's Epithet *Agonistes*," *Studies in English Literature*, IV (1964), pp. 137-62, a long and difficult essay, it finds the most illuminating meaning of epithet to be Samson's "playing a part," as he plays before and with the Philistines.